INSTITUTE OF PSYCHIATRY
Maudsley Monographs

MAUDSLEY MONOGRAPHS

HENRY MAUDSLEY, from whom the series of monographs takes its name, was the founder of the Maudsley Hospital and the most prominent English psychiatrist of his generation. The Maudsley Hospital was united with the Bethlem Royal Hospital in 1948, and its medical school, renamed the Institute of Psychiatry at the same time, became a constituent part of the British Postgraduate Medical Federation. It is entrusted by the University of London with the duty to advance psychiatry by teaching and research.

The monograph series reports work carried out in the Institute and in the associated Hospital. Some of the monographs are directly concerned with clinical problems; others, less obviously relevant, are in scientific fields that are cultivated for the furtherance of psychiatry.

INSTITUTE OF PSYCHIATRY
Maudsley Monographs
Number Twenty-Nine

The Natural History of Psychiatric Disorder in Children

*A study of individuals known to have attended both
Child and Adult Psychiatric Departments
of the same hospital*

By

H. ZEITLIN BSc, MPhil, MD, MRCP, FRCPsych.
*Senior Lecturer, Department of Child Psychiatry
Charing Cross and Westminster Medical School*

OXFORD UNIVERSITY PRESS
1986

Oxford University Press, Walton Street, Oxford OX2 6DP
Oxford New York Toronto
Delhi Bombay Calcutta Madras Karachi
Petaling Jaya Singapore Hong Kong Tokyo
Nairobi Dar es Salaam Cape Town
Melbourne Auckland
and associated companies in
Beirut Berlin Ibadan Nicosia

Oxford is a trade mark of Oxford University Press

Published in the United States
by Oxford University Press, New York

British Library Cataloguing in Publication Data
Zeitlin, H.
The Natural History of
Psychiatric disorders in children: a study of
individuals known to have attended both child and
adult psychiatric departments of the same hospital.
— (Institute of Psychiatry Maudsley monographs;
no. 29)
1. Child psychiatry — Cases, clinical reports,
statistics
I. Title   II. Series
618.92'89'09   RJ499
ISBN 0-19-712153-5

Library of Congress Cataloging in Publication Data
Zeitlin, H.
The Natural History of
Psychiatric disorders in children.
(Maudsley monographs; no. 29)
Bibliography: p.
Includes indexes.
1. Child psychopathology — Great Britain — Longitudinal
studies. 2. Mental illness — Forecasting. 3. Psych-
iatric hospital care — Great Britain — Longitudinal
studies. I. Title. II. Series. [DNLM: 1. Follow-Up
Studies. 2. Hospitals, Psychiatric — Great Britain.
3. Mental Disorders — in adulthood. 4. Mental Disorders —
in infancy & childhood. W1 MA997 no. 29/WS 350 Z48p]
RJ499.Z39   1986   618.92'89   86-2449
ISBN 0-19-712153-5

Set by Cotswold Typesetting Ltd, Cheltenham
Printed in Great Britain
at the University Printing House, Oxford
by David Stanford
Printer to the University

Preface

Child psychiatry is an area of study that has only recently been separated from adult psychiatry (Kanner, 1959; Warren, 1971). Earlier writers did make some note of the relationship between childhood and later mental health. Burton (1628) wrote of the Causes of Melancholy 'for if a man escapes a bad nurse, he may be undone by evil bringing up' and also '... (he) complains of a rigorous school master in Paris that made him ... once in a mind to drown himself'. Parkinson (1807) wrote on 'Excessive indulgence of children', and Johnson (1836) said 'Half and more than half of our miseries, crimes and misfortunes in after life are attributable to the misplaced indulgences or culpable negligence of our parents'. These authors commented mainly on environmental influence on development and later mental health. The phenomenology of child psychiatric disturbance received less attention, though as early as 1622 Baddeley described a boy of 13 with 'feigned madness'. During the nineteenth century more interest was shown, and Brigham (1839) stated that 'Children do not to be sure become insane, though they do occasionally from strong mental excitement ... But though mental excitement may not often produce insanity during childhood, it may predispose a person to this terrible disease'.

The development towards the end of the nineteenth century of individual psychology and of psychoanalysis with Freud's concepts of infant sexuality (Freud, 1905) led to increasing interest in childhood psychopathology. Freud even commented on his own daughter's natural progression to the analysis of children (Freud, 1933). In spite of the importance of childhood to Freud's concepts, he still had difficulty with the relationship between childhood and adult pathology. He stated, in terms remarkably similar to those of Brigham almost 100 years earlier:

'A great many children in these early years pass through conditions which may be compared with neuroses, and this is certainly true of those who develop the illness later on. In not a few cases the neurotic illness does not wait till they are grown up but breaks out in childhood'. This quotation from Freud raises questions that are as yet unanswered. Are childhood psychiatric disorders comparable with adult disorders or are there at least some that are special to childhood? If so what happens to these in adult life? Are there differences between adult disorders preceded by childhood disturbance and those that are not?

Child psychiatry is still at an early stage in its development and until recently speculation and retrospection from adult life were the main sources of theory. However, there is now a growing body of research and observations which can give some clue as to the natural history and prognosis from childhood into adult life (Rutter, 1978). Longitudinal research over many years presents hazards, but findings from various types of studies are now beginning to build a composite picture, and the case records at the Maudsley and Bethlem Hospital, linking the children's and adults' departments give a valuable opportunity to add to this. Though adult fantasies of childhood are vital to the understanding and treatment of adult psychopathology, the planning of educational, social, and psychiatric services must be based on direct observation and some understanding of the influence of real childhood events on future development. Klerman (1976) was concerned that current social influences on the young will predispose to a high rate of depression when this generation becomes old. He predicted (on little evidence), that 'We will be entering a new age of melancholy . . .'.

London   H. Z.
January 1986

Acknowledgements

The study presented here formed the basis of an MD Thesis presented to the University of London. I am indebted to Professor Michael Rutter who suggested the original project and who has since given continuous advice and support. I am particularly grateful for his meticulous examination of earlier drafts. Dr S Mann and Dr M Crowe acted as independent assessors for the diagnostic categories taking time and trouble to make the ratings as valid as possible. During the data collection the records department of the Maudsley Hospital gave every assistance in spite of interference with their normal heavy workload. I must thank also Mr P Nicholls for help with statistical analysis and Dr David Preston for access to computer facilities. Finally, my thanks to Mrs J Smith for her help and care in typing the manuscript.

Contents

Tables, diagrams, and graphs

1. Review of the literature

That 'the child is father to the man' seems in a general sense to be undisputed, but empirical research is now revealing a very complex interaction between the child and environment and many theories of normal or abnormal development are proving inadequate (Rutter, 1984a, b). Some of the information comes from studies of the long term outcome of childhood disorder (Robinson, 1951; Moore *et al.*, 1954; O'Neal & Robins, 1958; Robins, 1979; Rutter, 1984a), but such studies themselves present methodological difficulties (Rutter, 1982) and their limitations must be recognized. They cannot give direct information on developmental issues or on the aetiology of all psychiatric disorder, but longitudinal studies can help clarify such issues as classification, prevalence, and, of course, prognosis from childhood.

The continuities and discontinuities between child and adult disorder can be viewed either prospectively or retrospectively as the outcome from childhood or as the antecedents of adult disorder, but for each what is a suitable starting point? For adult disorder existing categories are far from satisfactory (Crowe *et al.*, 1979; Paykel & Rowan, 1979) but are generally accepted. Unfortunately for childhood disorders, with few exceptions, there is as yet insufficient information to identify clear nosological entities or even to confirm that they exist. Earlier theoretically based classifications merely produced a multiplicity of systems (Langford, 1964; GAP report, 1966). The two main classifications now used are that from the WHO study (Rutter *et al.*, 1969, 1975) and the American DSM III (Russell *et al.*, 1979). These are similar but with some important differences (Rutter & Shaffer, 1980). Both of these use as an essential part operationally defined 'syndromes', and Rutter (Rutter, 1965) specified some of the criteria for categories, particularly that 'they must be shown to differ in terms of aetiology, symptomatology, course, response to treatment or some other variable, other than the symptoms that define them'. Symptoms themselves must be considered epiphenomena and it cannot be assumed that any one symptom always has the same significance. Longitudinal research can help in two respects, first whether some symptoms have a constant course over time, and secondly whether symptom groupings have a validity in terms of outcome.

Following the course of any given symptom is more complicated than at first apparent, with possible differences in longitudinal course for the symptom alone, in the simultaneous presence of other but unconnected symptoms and as part of a constant cluster. The evidence so far is unclear; Wolff (1961), for example, originally grouped symptoms observed in 33 children into broad categories such as 'bad or unmanageable' and 'habit disorder', the first including both tantrums and overactivity. A recent follow-up study, however, indicated that these are independent items (August *et al.*, 1983). Various other examples can be cited; there are doubts about the significance and course of childhood misery (Graham, 1974, 1981); childhood fears for the most part do not persist and some seem to have very different prognostic significance (Shepherd *et al.*, 1966; Rutter & Garmezy, 1983); aggression is described by West and Farrington (1977) as being an important symptom, perhaps having a different significance from other antisocial behaviour and meriting more attention; obsessional disorders are generally agreed to have a bad prognosis, but whether a symptom complex is needed to define the disorder or whether the symptom alone is enough remains a matter of dispute (Judd, 1965; Adams, 1973; Hollingworth, *et al.*, 1980).

The search for empirical evidence for symptom clusters has also met with difficulties that can be helped by longitudinal research. Attempts have been made over a long period of time to search for valid factors or clusters of symptoms (Hewitt & Jenkins, 1946; Jenkins & Glickman, 1946; Collins & Maxwell, 1962; Dreger, 1964; Wolff, 1971). The greatest problem has been that whilst clusters of symptoms can be found, the symptoms in any one child are rarely 'pure' to any one cluster (Wolff, 1971). Wolff identified five factors: 1. aggressive acting out; 2. manifest anxiety; 3. antisocial behaviour; 4. depression and inhibition; 5. disturbance of toilet functioning; She found that most children scored on more than one. More consistently a distinction has been found between symptoms identified as emotional and those designated conduct disorder, but again mixed symptomatology is common. Such mixtures of symptoms do not, though, invalidate the findings but pose the question; do the mixtures represent entities in themselves or the co-existence of more than one disorder?

In spite of the uncertainties of currently used 'diagnostic' categories some of the data available on specific types of disorder also raise issues that might be answered by this type of study.

SCHIZOPHRENIA

For adults with psychotic illness there has been a move to use more precise and widely agreed operational definitions, whilst accepting that the then defined syndrome probably represents a spectrum of disorders (Crowe *et al.*, 1979). Crowe commented that outcome studies have been disappointing in differentiating types or aspects of this disorder. Can links with childhood help? First, about half of all individuals who develop schizophrenia do not show any apparent disturbance in child-hood (Rutter, 1984a). By the same account half do, and these may be divided into those who show symptoms identifiable as the adult form and those who show 'clearly abnormal, albeit non-psychotic patterns of behaviour in childhood'.

Most authors agree that typical schizophrenia does occur in children, though uncommonly below age 13 and rarely below age 7 (Rutter, 1972c; Eggers, 1978). Kolvin and colleagues (1971) and Eggers (1978) both noted, though, that the 'typical' symptoms had their own form and were less elaborate, the earlier the developmental stage.

As stated, such presentation is at best uncommon and far more present with so-called non-psychotic symptoms in childhood. A variety of claims have been made for such antecedents, including withdrawal (Bower, 1960) neurotic symptoms (Wittman, 1944; Gardener, 1967), poor academic achievement (Schofield, 1959), and aggressiveness (Morris *et al.*, 1956). What now seems to emerge is a pattern of symptoms that otherwise less commonly occur together. The pattern has several elements (Rutter, 1984a): 1. a mixture of emotional symptoms of depression, overdependence, and being ruminative, together with antisocial behaviour that is not carried out with peers but is instead against them and the family (Frazee, 1953; Robins, 1966); 2. relationship difficulties with social isolation (Frazee, 1953; Lewine *et al.*, 1980; Rutter & Garmezy, 1983); 3. poor school record and educational functioning (Robins, 1966; Schofield, 1959; Bower, 1960). This derives from several factors, apart from the behavioural and relationship problems, as various neurological, developmental and perceptual deficits, as well as attention deficits have been found (Fish, 1960; Kolvin *et al.*, 1971; Rutter & Garmezy, 1983; Rutter, 1984a).

None of these elements is a specific antecedent of schizophrenia, nor is it clear whether they are absent from those who develop overt psychosis in childhood or whether groups differ only in the presence or absence of more clearly defined psychotic symptoms.

Not all researchers have found neurodevelopmental disorders in the childhood of future schizophrenics (Hanson *et al.*, 1976). Their results may be due purely to methodological differences from other studies, as they were assessing children of schizophrenic parents, but this does raise the possibility of sub-groups with and without such neurological con-comitants.

DEPRESSION

Depression is one of the commonest diagnoses made in adults though uncertainty remains about different types of this disorder (Paykel &

Rowan, 1979). A variety of terms are used to designate apparent entities, implying differences in severity, biological and psychological dysfunction, and aetiology. A detailed discussion of these would be out of place here but a distinction between two forms of adult depression is supported by data from studies of child/adult continuities. The first may be described as typical affective psychosis and the second as 'other depression'.

AFFECTIVE PSYCHOSIS*

There are continual reports that in childhood affective psychosis is often overlooked or misdiagnosed (Campbell, 1955; Annell, 1969; Weinberg & Brumback, 1976; Makita, 1974; August *et al.*, 1983; Conners, 1976). The problem centres largely on the criteria that would be appropriate for diagnosis. Weinberg and Brumback (1976) stressed family history but in the five cases they reported there is little account either of the nature of the parental illness or of the degree to which the children were directly involved in the parent's symptoms. They also listed the symptom criteria but these were comprehensive and would be difficult to see as being specific to this relatively uncommon disorder. Their symptom list was, for example, remarkably like that given by Gross and Wilson (1974) for minimal brain damage. It is interesting that both of these groups of authors used the same range of drugs in treatment. It may be that the children were all showing the same disorder, but some other criterion is needed to indicate whether this is in any way equivalent to adult affective psychosis. Annell (1969) actually used response to treatment with Lithium as a diagnostic criterion in children in whom she felt that the psychosis was masked by other symptoms. This would seem hazardous and in any case eleven of her twelve cases were over the age of 13 at the start of treatment. There are no clear-cut reports of prepubertal children being given this diagnosis and then followed into adult life to show the pattern of disorder. In contrast to this, Angst and colleagues (1973) reported on the age of onset of affective psychosis and a further appraisal of his data (Angst, 1975) showed that none of his cases had commenced before the age of 16. It was unclear whether patients had shown any symptoms without referral, but Dahl (1971) looked at childhood records of adults with manic-depressive illness and found nothing other than chance association. Evidence is therefore still lacking to show a continuity between child disorder and adult manic-depressive illness.

A slightly different issue arises concerning those teenagers who symptomatically show a definite psychotic disorder. It seems that

*Affective psychosis is used as being synonymous with manic-depressive psychosis and refers to monopolar and bipolar conditions unless otherwise stated.

schizophrenic illness and manic-depressive psychosis may be difficult to distinguish in this age range (Creak, 1962; Steinberg, 1983). This is important as both conditions are frequently treated using either depot preparations of drugs or a long-term regimen of medication. The drugs used, though, are different (Steinberg, 1983) and each may mask symptoms, come what may. More research is needed to help distinguish these conditions or show that the passage of time is necessary to clarify a diagnosis.

OTHER AFFECTIVE DISORDERS

The majority of adults with depression have shown no childhood antecedents (Huffman, 1954; Pritchard & Graham, 1966), but, for those who have, relatively little is known about the links, if any, between the childhood disorder and adult depression.

In the past, many symptoms have been attributed to depression in childhood but it is only recently that attempts have been made to define syndromes of childhood depression (Pearce, 1974, 1977; Kashani *et al.*, 1981; Kovacs *et al.*, 1984; Puig-Antich & Gittelman, 1982). Pearce (1974, 1977), in a study of children attending the Maudsley Hospital, found that certain symptoms did show significant association with depressed mood, and both Puig-Antich and Gittelman (1982) and Kovacs and colleagues (1984) have identified what they believe to be depressive syndromes in children similar to those found in adults. But what happens to these syndromes? Do they ever continue to the same disorder in adult life? Poznanski (1980) proposed that children 'do not outgrow depression' but offered little evidence, and though Puig-Antich is using long-term outcome as one parameter in his study results are not yet available. One group (Eastgate & Gilmore, 1984) reported a variable and unfavourable outcome in some cases, but as depression often appears with other symptoms such as conduct disorder (Kolvin & Nicol, 1979; Rutter, 1984a) their prognosis may depend more on the coexisting symptoms.

Overt depression is generally agreed to be less common in middle childhood (Cytryn & McKnew, 1974) and a variety of explanations has been put forward for this. Among these is the concept of masked depression, that is to say that the 'mechanism' of depression occurs, but is manifest by phenomena other than mood change. At one time this concept found strong support but has tended more recently to go out of favour, though Puig-Antich (Puig-Antich & Gittelman, 1982) considers that it merits further research. The symptoms proposed have included the following: delinquency and aggression (Drotar, 1974; Lesse, 1974), somatic symptoms and abdominal pain (Frommer & Cottom, 1970), headaches (Ling *et al.*, 1970), enuresis (Sacks, 1974), hyperactivity (Cytryn & McKnew, 1974), and school refusal (Agras, 1959). In the absence of an identifiable underlying mechanism, one way of testing this would be to look for any symptoms that show continuity with later adult depression. This would not prove that the childhood symptoms were the same condition but would be a step towards it. So far no research findings are available on this.

EMOTIONAL DISORDERS/NEUROTIC DISORDER

The term neurosis or neurotic disorder was originally used to imply organic disorder of the nerves (Cullen, 1784) but is now used to include 'generally maladaptive behaviour in which there is no organic basis and in which reality testing is unimpaired' (Marks, 1973). For children the term emotional disorder tends to be favoured, largely to avoid the implication of direct comparability with adult neurosis (Hersov, 1977b). As earlier noted, psychoanalytic writings have assumed a link between 'childhood neurosis' and 'adult neurosis' (Freud, 1933), but the empirical data concerning overt symptoms in children bring this into question.

The links between childhood emotional disorder and adult neurosis have been reviewed by several authors (Rutter, 1971, 1984a; Marks, 1973) and some consistent findings are apparent. First, most studies report a good prognosis for emotional disorders as a whole (Masterson, 1967; Lo, 1973; Robins, 1979). Lo (1973) found that at follow-up at 3 years 78.6 per cent of neurotic children were improved, as compared with 53.3 per cent of behaviour disorder, and in Robins' study (Robins, 1966) children diagnosed as neurotic were no more likely to have adult psychiatric problems than were controls. Secondly, though emotionally disturbed children are not especially predisposed to develop adult illness, a pattern of response is established, so that should they become ill, the adult illness will be of a neurotic nature, rather than antisocial or psychotic (Pritchard & Graham 1966; Mellsop, 1973). The definition of neurotic disorders results in the inclusion of a variety of symptoms and there is less clear evidence about whether the nature of the emotional symptoms will be the same in childhood and adult life.

The wide mixture of symptoms included in the overall group of emotional disorders presents particular problems. The frequent co-existence of symptoms does not indicate that they necessarily have to occur together or that they are the result of the same underlying mechanism. Depression and obsessions are two particular examples where there is some evidence to support their separation from the main group of emotional disorders. Longitudinal studies so far have tended not to provide any separate category for childhood depression (Pritchard & Graham, 1966; Robins, 1966; Mellsop, 1973), and the childhood symptoms are usually included in the overally emotional group.

Obsessional disorders are particularly different with regard to outcome. Though the overall prognosis is good for emotional disorders, this is not so for obsessions; Pollitt (1957) found that two-thirds of all cases had previous attacks in childhood and adolescence, while Lo (1967) studying obsessive compulsive neurosis in Hong Kong found that 12.5 per cent presented before age 11 and 33 per cent gave a history of childhood symptoms. In a prospective study (Hollingworth *et al.*, 1980) ten out of seventeen children still had symptoms at a mean follow up period of 6.5 years.

In spite of this very important difference, Judd (1965) and Adams (1973) required other emotional symptoms to be present to define an obsessional syndrome. Though the other symptoms may have a special significance if they occur in the presence of obsessions there is nothing to indicate this. It is of interest that most outcome studies have looked for the symptom alone at follow-up, in spite of requiring a syndrome to start.

A further group that shows difference from the body of emotional disorder concerns those children refusing to go to school (Rutter, 1984a). Certainly the syndrome of school refusal includes generalized anxiety and anxiety related to specific circumstances and misery, but the prognosis is again worse than for other emotional disorders (Coolidge *et al.*, 1964; Hersov, 1977b). The nature of the outcome in adult life is usually reported as involving work difficulty and relationship problems, though there is some evidence of a discontinuity to a different focus for the adult fear (Berg *et al.*, 1974b; Tyrer & Tyrer, 1974). Here again more research is needed concerning outcome.

CONDUCT DISORDER/PERSONALITY DISORDER

The final type of symptoms to be considered is those that are regarded as aggressive or antisocial. In adult life these are usually deemed to be part of a personality disorder, though the whole concept of personality disorder is complex (Rutter, 1984b) and any subclassification into different types proves unreliable (Tyrer & Alexander, 1979). The associations with childhood are particularly important as personality disorder appears almost always to commence early in life (Robins, 1978; Rutter & Garmezy, 1983; Rutter, 1984a).

Some consistent findings do arise from the literature. First, there has long been a consistent separation between emotional disorder and conduct disorder, particularly in research using factor analysis (Jenkins

& Glickman, 1946; Collins & Maxwell, 1962; Wolff, 1971). Most subsequent research has supported the separation when these symptoms occur in children who show only one or the other (Wolff, 1973; Rutter, 1978), but has also shown a considerable overlap, and the significance of these patterns of behaviour is far from clear when they coexist (Rutter, 1978). Secondly, without exception, available studies give a bad prognosis for children with conduct disorder, those who would be deemed delinquent having the worst outlook (Glueck & Glueck, 1940; Pritchard & Graham, 1966; Morris *et al.*, 1956; Robins, 1978; Mulligan *et al.*, 1963; Masterson, 1967; Lo, 1973; West & Farrington, 1977). This prognosis is that children with antisocial behaviour are more likely to show adult disorder compared with 'normal' controls (O'Neal & Robins, 1958) or other clinic children, other than those with overt psychosis (Pritchard & Graham, 1966). None the less, antisocial behaviour is more common in childhood and, of all conduct disordered children, a large proportion of those with antisocial behaviour will make a satisfactory adjustment in adult life. Two issues follow from this, how to tell which children will have adult disorder, and if they have adult disorder, what will be its nature.

Several indicators of poor prognosis have emerged, mostly relating to pervasiveness. This refers to the number and variety of antisocial symptoms present (Annesley, 1961; Robins, 1966), to the range of situations in which antisocial behaviour is manifest, patients showing such behaviour outside home being more at risk (West & Farrington, 1977; Rutter, 1984a), and to its persistence over time. A further finding that follows from this is that those involved with the law in childhood have a high likelihood of reconviction as adults. Adult conviction rates as high as 80 per cent have been found (Glueck & Glueck, 1940) but West & Farrington (1977) found a rate of 61 per cent and Robins (1966) of 58 per cent, the latter compared with 14 per cent of non-delinquent controls.

Developmental delays are constantly found linked to conduct disorder in childhood (Rutter, Tizard & Whitmore, 1970), but whether this is a factor related to long term outcome is uncertain, though Rutter (1984b) suggested that the association of conduct disorder with attention deficits, impulsiveness, and overactivity is.

Three further types of influence may be considered in sequence: genetic factors, early character traits, and 'the family'. Though genetic influences may have a predisposing effect the evidence seems to be that they play only a minor role in determining outcome (Rutter, 1984a). Early character traits have been linked to childhood disorder (Thomas *et al.*, 1963) and to adult psychiatric disorder (Schulsinger, 1972; Bronson, 1967; Livson & Peskin, 1967) but probably also play only a minor part

(Rutter, 1984a). These two factors in any case require very different research design. Many aspects of family life have been implicated in the genesis of childhood conduct disorder, including parental discord, parental criminality, lack of affection, and absence of parents. Whether these family factors occurring in childhood continue to have an adverse affect on mental health into adult life is uncertain except, perhaps, for the evidence for an association between early parental loss and personality disorder (Bowlby *et al.*, 1956; Earle & Earle, 1961; West & Farrington, 1977).

There are many unanswered questions concerning the links between childhood disturbance and adult psychiatric disorder and this review has taken a brief look at some of the aspects that might be clarified by longitudinal research.

FOLLOW-UP STUDIES

Information on the links between child and adult disorder comes from many different types of study. The simplest method of trying to obtain data over a long period of time in the same individual is by asking that person to recollect past events. For a long time this method has been traditional in psychiatry (Freud, 1901; Barry, 1936; Jung, 1954; Kerr *et al.*, 1972). However, Freud himself was aware that this mainly gives information about the current meaning of the recollection (Freud, 1901, p. 46 et seq.). There are many reasons why this is an unreliable means of testing the significance of events that actually did take place (Yarrow *et al.*, 1970), including distortions in reporting (Chess *et al.*, 1966) and the effects of illness on recall (Wardell & Balinson, 1964). Barraclough & Bunch (1973) found that time alone rapidly decreased the accuracy of recall of such 'hard data' as year of death of a parent.

More objective techniques use contemporary data (recorded at the time of occurrence) provided by someone other than the subject, and the conceptual and methodological problems have been reviewed by various authors (Moore *et al.*, 1954; Wardell & Balinson, 1964; Robins, 1979; Rutter, 1972a, 1977a, 1982). Most studies deal either with whole populations and short-term follow-up (cross-sectional studies) or selected populations and long-term follow-up (follow-up studies). Burt (1937) was one of the first to carry out a cross-sectional study but more recently some very meticulous research has been carried out examining all children in a given population. Rutter and his colleagues (Rutter *et al.*, 1970) screened all 10-year-olds on the Isle of Wight for a wide variety of emotional, behavioural, educational, and physical phenomena, following them up 4–5 years later (Graham & Rutter, 1973); subsequently, they performed a similar exercise in an inner London borough (Rutter *et al.*, 1975). Shepherd (Shepherd *et al.*, 1971) charted the prevalence of behavioural phenomena in school children of various ages in Buckinghamshire but, though these studies are valuable for information on prevalence, they cannot be used as a series of cross-sections to build a composite picture over time. That requires information about phenomena at different points in the life of each individual.

Some studies have attempted to take samples of whole populations and follow them through life. Those initiated by Douglas (Douglas & Mulligan, 1961; Douglas, 1966) and the National Children's Bureau (Pringle *et al.*, 1966) are examples. Though ambitious and time-consuming, these are best able to give information about the distribution of a given factor or measure in a whole population and the National Children's Bureau study has reported such items as mortality rates, effects of family size, and social class, (Davie *et al.*, 1972). The items studied can be related to some index of disturbance to evaluate vulnerability or risk, but whole-population surveys are relatively poor tools for the study of different types of disorder unless that disorder has very high prevalence (Garmezy, 1974). Even with high prevalence, the very bulk of data yielded by widely based studies makes more detailed examination of disorder arduous. West (West, 1969; West & Farrington, 1977) was able to study delinquency in a sample of 411 schoolboys largely because over 30 per cent had shown delinquent behaviour within fourteen years, and he concentrated on that type of behaviour. More specific samples may be selected on such criteria as clinic attendance (Morris *et al.*, 1954; Rodriguez *et al.*, 1959; Warren, 1965) or symptoms or conditions such as school refusal (Coolidge *et al.*, 1964). The conclusions drawn must be applied to the sample and not to the whole population, though use of suitable control groups helps with interpretation of the data (Robins, 1966; Zeitlin, 1971).

Longer-term follow-up is a daunting task as part of a single research project. Robinson (1951) made a personal approach to 45 subjects seen by herself 25 years earlier and though the descriptions are interesting they do not lend themselves to systematic analysis. Robins (1979) pointed out that for follow-up studies it is essential to have data collected at at least two points in time, but those data do not have to be obtained by the same person, provided that they have been systematically collected and clearly recorded. Past records of selected populations are invaluable in this respect and can be used in various ways.

Data may be available on a selected group which is then followed for outcome. The now classical study of Robins (1966) is such an example. Robins and her co-workers chanced upon the old records from a clinic specializing in referrals from the Courts. They succeeded in tracing some

90 per cent of the individuals concerned, in adult life. In another study, Bronson (1967) was able to make use of the research records of 66 individuals obtained more than 20 years earlier (Macfarlane *et al.*, 1954). Such studies give clearest information about the outcome of a given characteristic or disorder, and better sample size for a given outcome can be obtained by identifying a group at point of outcome and searching for early records. Several studies of this nature have been carried out, for example for adults with schizophrenia (Wittman, 1948; Waring & Ricks, 1965; Offord & Cross, 1971), but it is rare to find a single source of early data that is reliable.

In a few instances detailed records have been made at two points in a person's life under reasonably standardized conditions (Frazee, 1953; Pritchard & Graham, 1966; Zeitlin, 1971; Mellsop, 1972). The populations studied are highly selected there being criteria for selection at both points in time, but the data can, none the less, be used to demonstrate correlations that might occur, based either on outcome from childhood data or on the antecedents of adult data. With the use of suitable adult and child controls it is possible to investigate whether childhood disorders have an outcome differing from those disorders that originate in adult life, and also whether the childhood antecedents of adult disorder differ from disorder existing only in childhood.

2. The study

The main purpose of the study was to examine the links between overt child and adult psychiatric disorders when both had occurred in the same individual. Any findings could be considered both in terms of the antecedents of adult disorder and the outcome of child disorder. To achieve this aim some preliminary tasks had to be accomplished. First, to identify a group in which there were reliable data at both points in the person's life; secondly, to establish items of information that were recorded in a sufficiently routine manner to be available in the majority of records, and thirdly to extract the data in such a way that any further 'recording bias' was reduced to a minimum. Once a series of standardized files was obtained, various hypotheses or statements could be made and tested from the data. Before looking at continuities, though, it was necessary to see whether people in this index group differed, either in the manifest phenomena or in life circumstances, from those with illness at one point only. Specific control or comparison groups therefore had to be established. The final step was to test for the proposed continuities within the index group itself. This again could be split into several specific questions; do continuities exist (a) for recognized diagnostic categories, (b) for individual items, and (c) for broader categories other than diagnoses used? If any continuities are found then, unless these are absolute, a final question is whether there are identifiable differences between those with continuity of illness and those without?

Appropriate information was to be found recorded in the case notes of the children's and adult departments in the Maudsley and Bethlem Hospitals. The children's department started over 50 years ago, so that many of the patients who have attended are now adult and it was apparent from the adult department that at least some had returned with further psychiatric problems.

For many years the hospital has been a training establishment. Soon after the development of the children's department, it began to use systematic and standardized methods of history-taking and case-note recording, which have changed little over the subsequent years. As a result the case notes provide a source of detailed information that is standard from record to record and for those who attended both in childhood and adult life the information is available at two points in time. These records therefore conform to the recommendations of Robins (1966) as a source of data for a follow-up study.

Those cases with attendance both in childhood and adult life formed the index group, and several types of control groups were identified. From the perspective of childhood it was necessary to see how these compared with other children who attended but did not have adult disorder, and from the adult perspective a comparison group was required of adults who had no childhood disturbance. These two control groups would have to be matched for sex and age with the index cases but, as age and sex distribution of the sample is important, further comparison had to be made with all children attending the children's department over the same period of time. This latter 'group' was designated Control group I, and the two matched groups, were designated Control groups II and III respectively. Age and sex comparisons for the index cases in adult life could be made against the available Maudsley Hospital statistics.

SELECTION OF INDEX CASES

Each new referral of the same person is recorded separately and a new front page identification sheet is used in the case notes for each three-year period. Using these identification sheets a search was made through all adult records for a six-year period from 1964 to 1969, for anyone who had previously attended the Maudsley Hospital children's department. In all, 327 cases were identified and, of these, 307 sets of case notes were located.

Exclusions from the study were made on the following criteria.

(a) Attendance in childhood for epilepsy only.
(b) Attendance in childhood for mental handicap only.
(c) IQ below 60 irrespective of reason for referral.
(d) First attendance in children's department after 1961.
(e) First attendance after 16th birthday.
(f) Immediate referral from children's department to adult department.
(g) Inadequate records.

Of the 307 case notes examined, 146 eventually failed to meet the criteria. The majority of exclusions, 101 cases, were on grounds of being over 16 at referral to the children's department or because of rapid transfer from children's department to the adult department (exclusion criteria d, e & f). In 13 cases attendance was for epilepsy only and a further 15 were excluded because of mental handicap (criteria b & c); 17 cases were not used because of scanty or inadequate information in adult records.

The 161 cases remaining constituted the index group. In all of them there was a minimum 2-year gap between childhood attendance and first adult attendance and a minimum follow-up period from first childhood attendance of 5 years (this resulted from exclusion criteria d, e & f).

CONTROL GROUP I

This group consisted of all children attending the same children's department between 1946 and 1961. The data were obtained from the new case registers in the children's department and the same age limits were used as for index cases. Comparison with this control was only for age and sex distribution.

CONTROL GROUP II: THE CHILD CONTROLS

A second control group was matched for age, sex, and date of childhood attendance and was used for all other index control comparisons in childhood. The group was located by tracing each index case in the children's department case register and then locating the next child of the same age and sex to attend. If forward tracing failed to identify a suitable control within six months of date of birth and six months of attendance, a search was made in the immediately previous six-month period. Exclusions were made on the same basis as the index cases or if the case was subsequently known to have attended elsewhere as an adult. In fifteen cases this was apparent from letters requesting information.

CONTROL GROUP III: THE ADULT CONTROLS

The third group of controls were matched for age, sex, and date of first attendance as adults, and was used for all index control comparisons in adult life. Rejection for use as an adult control was made on the following criteria:

(a) Onset of illness prior to age 16.
(b) Known attendance for any reason at any department of child psychiatry.
(c) Record of contact with any agency as a result of disturbed behaviour during childhood.
(d) An account of any major symptoms prior to age 16 in the past history of the adult.
(e) Inadequate case record.

All adult records over the same period of time were used as a source of controls and three possible cases were selected for each index case. In all, some 413 sets of notes were examined, and the largest number of exclusions, about two-thirds, made on the grounds of evidence of manifest symptoms prior to age 16. Of the remainder the majority were rejected because of inadequate recorded data. Six sets of notes could not be traced.

The difficulty in finding suitable adult controls is important to the study as a whole. At first view the index group appears to be highly selected, but as some 40 per cent of the adult records examined had symptoms in childhood the results of the study are relevant to a sizeable proportion of all adult psychiatric patients.

DATA ABSTRACTION

A preliminary study was made of twenty-three case notes in order to plan a proforma for the abstraction of data. Forty-three symptoms from the childhood record and forty from the adult record were selected for use. A category of 'other' was included with each to safeguard against the omission of any frequently occurring or significant symptom. The rest of the proforma included items concerning the nature of the referral, family life and structure, development and cognitive functioning. Operational definitions were made for all items used and a manual was prepared for guidance in data abstraction. Index and control records were examined in random order and in each index case the childhood and adult records were examined at different times.

DIAGNOSIS

For each case a research diagnosis was allocated for the childhood and adult attendances. In childhood one scale was used based on the first axis of the WHO classification (Rutter *et al.*, 1969). The scale used a 'normal' point and two diagnostic categories could be used for each child (Appendix II). For adults two scales were used (Appendix II), the first based on the ICD and the second separately classifying personality disorder. In addition to the proforma data, detailed case summaries were available to assist diagnostic ratings.

The case records were examined by two clinicians, i.e. the author, HZ, plus one other, MC, for child records, and SM for adult records. Disagreement occurred in 40 per cent of child diagnoses and 25 per cent of adult diagnoses, though for child cases there was initial agreement in over 70 per cent for at least one diagnostic label. Most of the differences centred on distinguishing between conduct disorder and delinquency and on the possibility that more than two diagnostic labels were applicable. For the adult diagnostic labels there was better agreement; nearly all differences concerned the type of personality disorder or the type of neurotic disorder (rather than whether one or the other was present).

Where disagreement occurred the case notes were examined by both assessors together until agreement was reached.

Case notes provide a very imprecise tool. In spite of the systematic case note recording at the Maudsley Hospital there is no means of testing the reliability of observations or the accuracy of recording. The fact that the records were made by many different clinicians raises questions of differences in interpretation of phenomena, but does also tend to reduce the likelihood of systematic error due to the idiosyncrasies of one person.

The child controls (Control group II) were selected from the same child population. Though every effort was made to exclude any case with later adult disturbance it is almost certain that some would have developed significant disorder in adult life, but presented elsewhere, no letter for information being filed in the notes. This group therefore provides an 'impure' control. However, its effect would reduce the probability of differences from the index group rather than cause spurious ones.

The adult controls all had detailed case histories, in many instances from several informants. It is possible that childhood symptoms occurred but were not recorded or were deliberately concealed by the informants, but the adult control group would seem to constitute a more precise control.

Of the 327 cases identified, 20 sets of notes were not located giving a 93.9 per cent tracing rate. Most authors record rates of between 90–95 per cent as very high (Robins, 1966; Sims, 1973; West & Farrington, 1977). In this instance the notes could not be located and it seems unlikely that there would be a systematic clinical reason for their absence. A check was made that they were not in current use elsewhere in the hospital. It is also likely that a proportion of those not traced would have been rejected on selection criteria.

The best known case-note study is that of Robins (1966). In that study 524 children were traced into adult life and compared with 100 controls. Follow-up interviews would have been desirable in this study but was beyond the scope of the investigation. Unlike Robins' study all index cases were known to have attended in adult life so that in spite of smaller numbers relatively more data is available concerning the relationship between child and adult disorder.

Pritchard and Graham (1966) carried out a case-note study on the same population, but studied only 64 children, comparing them on 17 items, and they made no comparison with controls. A further case-note follow-up study was reported from Melbourne in which a search was made for adult records of 3370 children (Mellsop, 1972, 1973) for whom childhood records were available. In all, 227 were located but of these 58 male and 43 female subjects were referred mainly for mental handicap. There was also no comparison with adult controls.

THE SAMPLE

Distribution according to sex

The ratio of male to female in the index group was 98:63 or 61 per cent male (Table 2.1). This differed little from the overall ratio for all children

Table 2.1. *Distribution of sample according to sex*

	Index group		Children 1949–58		Adults 1964–69	
	N	%	N	%	N	%
Male	98	61	2309	67	—	50.8
Female	63	39	1126	33	—	49.2
Total	161	100	3435	100	—	100

Figures for adults from Maudsley Hospital Triennial Statistics Index v. Adults χ^2 6.57, d.f.1, $p < 0.05$.

attending the clinic during the same period (67 per cent male), but showed a large difference to the ratio for adults which is almost 1:1.

The predominance of boys over girls found in this study is in accordance with other studies of child clinic populations. Various authors report ratios almost identical to those here (Rutter & Graham, 1966; Gardener, 1967; Sundby & Kreyberg, 1968), though others have found even higher proportions of boys at about 70 per cent to 75 per cent (Mellsop, 1973; Lo, 1973; Morris *et al.*, 1954; Robins, 1966). Some of the difference may be due to referral bias and in Robins' study the proportion of boys in those referred for antisocial problems was 75.6 per cent but for other types of disorder 69.3 per cent. The wide age range in this study may also account for a lower ratio as the proportion of girls rises in cases referred in adolescence (Mattison *et al.*, 1967).

Distribution according to age at first attendance

Graphs 2.1a, and 2.1b show the age distribution for boys and girls compared with control group I. If age 12 is used as a dividing line then for both sexes there is no statistical difference between index cases and controls for younger and older children (Table 2.2). The graph does show that there is however a higher proportion of girls in the oldest age group for the index cases and Table 2.2 also shows that for all children fewer females than males attended below the age of 12.

Table 2.2. *Age distribution of index cases compared with all cases attending between 1948–1961*

	Male Index cases	All male children 1949–61	Females Index cases	All female children 1949–61
Under 12	71	2291	31	1018
Over 12	27 (*27.6*)	1021 (*30.8*)	32 (*50.8*)	688 (*40.3*)
Total	98	3312	63	1701

Figures in brackets are percentages of column totals.
Index cases Male/Female χ^2 8.92 d.f.1, $p < 0.01$.

Distribution according to age at adult attendance

Table 2.3 shows that at the end of the follow-up period the majority of index cases were between ages 20–35 with almost a total absence of older patients.

The children attending the clinic ranged in age from 4 years to 15 years old, and Diagram 2.1 shows the effects of the selection criteria. No persons born after January 1954 could be included as they would not have reached their 16th birthday by the end of 1969. The shaded area on the diagram represents the children excluded on this basis, i.e. four-year-olds in 1958, four- and five-year-olds in 1959, and so forth. Because no children were below age 4 and because the proportion of clinic cases decreases with decreasing age (Graph 2.1a and b) the actual number of children excluded is likely to be quite small. For boys the age distributions of the index cases and all clinic referrals were very similar (Graph 2.1a and b). For girls the index group contained relatively more older children. It seems unlikely that this is due to the study design, as it

Table 2.3. *Age range of adult sample at last recorded notes*

Age	Index (N=98) (%)	All adult patients (N=5242) (%)	Index (N=63) (%)	All female patients (N=5197) (%)
16–19	19.4	11.5	7.9	11.2
20–24	37.8	16.8	41.3	16.8
25–34	35.7	27.7	38.1	24.4
35–44	6.1	20.8	11.1	19.6
45+	1.0	26.0	1.0	28.0

Male χ^2 58.72, d.f. 4, $p < 0.001$.
Female χ^2 39.02, d.f. 4, $p < 0.001$.

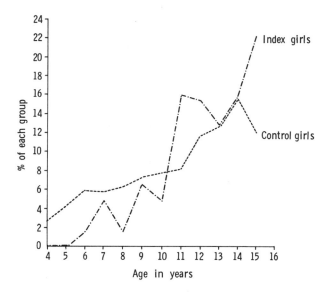

Graph 2.1 (a). Age distributions of index girls compared with all female children attending between 1949 and 1961 (N.B. for age exclusions see text.)

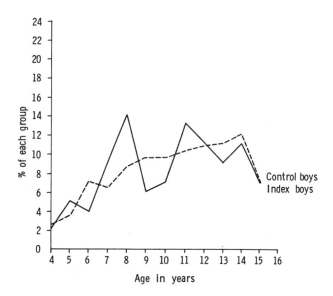

Graph 2.1 (b). Age distributions of index boys compared with all male children attending between 1949 and 1961 (N.B. for age exclusions see text.)

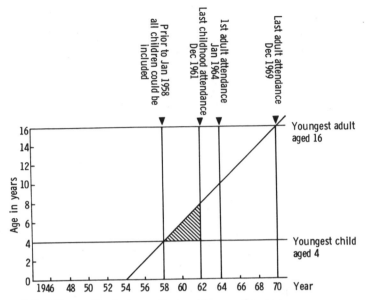

Diagram 2.1. Effects of inclusion criteria with regard to age.
Notes: (a) No child younger than four years found in sample.
     (b) No adult attendance at age less than 16 years.
     (c) Adult attendances Jan. 1964 to Dec. 1969.
     (d) Last childhood attendance Dec. 1961.
     (e) Minimum possible follow-up period: two years.

applies only to girls, or to a referral bias, as it would then also be found for all female referrals. The finding is therefore more likely to be a reflection of the nature of disorders persisting in girls into adult life.

The lack of elderly patients in the index group is a direct result of the limited period over which data was available, the longest follow-up period possible being 37 years. This does serve as a reminder that the data refer only to illness arising early in adult life and that there are virtually no studies on the relationship between childhood disorder and mental illness in later life.

3. Children with psychiatric disorder recurring in adult life: comparison with child controls

INDEX CASES IN CHILDHOOD

The index cases and the matched child control group are from the same clinic population, but the index cases were also selected by the later presence of disturbance in adult life. The advantage of this perspective in time was not available at childhood presentation and this chapter therefore seeks to identify any other criteria by which all or some of the index cases could be identified.

CLINIC ATTENDANCE

The children's clinic basically had two functions: assessment and treatment. It was the first of these functions that gave most information about the cases, but various factors can influence duration of attendance and outcome, including clinic policy, treatment techniques, severity and persistence of disorder, and parental concern and commitment.

In all, 55 per cent of the children, index and controls, attended for more than six months, but twice as many control boys attended for fewer than six months (control 37.6 per cent, index 17.7 per cent), and three times as many control girls as index girls (control 40.4 per cent, index 13.3 per cent) (Table 3.1).

After treatment was discontinued a number of children were referred again for further assessment and treatment. Table 3.1, showing duration of attendance, includes all such re-referrals and uses the time from first to last attendance, irrespective of discharge in between. Index boys and girls were also more likely to have more than one referral, as compared with the controls, the difference being significant at the 1 per cent level for boys. In the index group, though girls were less likely to be re-referred, as compared with index boys, this seems to have been compensated for by a longer duration of attendance.

One of the possible reasons for the longer duration of attendance is that the index cases showed severe disorder that persisted without remission into adult life. An attempt was made to classify the clinician's comments concerning change in the child by the time of last childhood

Table 3.1. *Duration of attendance*

	Boys		Girls	
	Index N (%)	Control N (%)	Index N (%)	Control N (%)
Attendance less than 6 months	19	43	11	29
Corrected for single appointment only	17 (*17.7*)	33 (*37.6*)	8 (*13.3*)	23 (*40.4*)
Attendance for more than 6 months	79 (*82.4*)	55 (*62.5*)	52 (*86.7*)	34 (*59.6*)

χ^2 Boys 9.09, d.f.1, $p < 0.001$.
χ^2 Girls 10.96, d.f.1, $p < 0.001$.
Figures in brackets give percentages of boys or girls who attended on two occasions or more.

attendance. The term 'recovered' was used to denote loss of symptoms together with overall better adjustment, often of the whole family; the term 'improved' usually meant loss of symptoms or decrease in severity to the extent that change was clearly thought to have taken place, though either some symptoms remained or it was unclear as to how satisfactory the final situation was.

On the criteria used for outcome, index boys did no worse than control boys and index girls appeared to do better (Table 3.2). This applied both to younger and older children. In spite of the longer duration of attendance for many of the index group, the contemporary clinicians do not appear to have predicted the future disturbance, at least in terms of pessimism at the end of the childhood attendance.

It is difficult to find data from other studies that are strictly comparable with this. Most other studies have looked at efficacy of treatment

Table 3.2. *Condition on discharge*

	Boys		Girls	
	Index N=98	Control N=98	Index N=63	Control N=63
Recovered or improved	67.8	47.9	79.3	53.9
No change or worse	30.5	36.7	14.2	33.3
Single attendance only	2.0	10.2	4.7	9.5

χ^2 Boys 2.81, d.f.1, NS.
χ^2 Girls 7.72, d.f.1, $p < 0.01$.
Figures shown are percentages of column totals.

and short term outcome. Though treatment may be associated with prolonged attendance it cannot be equated with it. It is also apparent from the findings here that short term and long term outcomes can be very different. Shepherd and colleagues (1966) compared children attending a clinic with children matched for symptomatology, but not referred or receiving treatment. At two-year follow-up they found the proportion improved to be the same in both groups. They also rated two years' outcome against the number of clinic attendances and concluded that there was no relationship. However, they found that of 18 attending for 5 or fewer sessions 15 (83.3 per cent) improved at two years compared with 53.6 per cent of the 28 who attended for six or more sessions. Though this falls short of statistical significance they had excluded psychosis and severe conduct disorder, but still found a pattern suggesting worse outcome for those attending longer. Robins' study (1966) unfortunately does not give any data specifically relating to duration of attendance but does indicate that those who showed repeated episodes of disturbed conduct were more likely to be future sociopaths. One difficulty in making a comparison is that clinic policy could have a major effect on the data. Malmivaara and colleagues (1975) found that at a 10-year follow-up longer duration of treatment was linked both with neurotic disorder and better outcome. However, neurotic or emotional disorder in childhood appears in any case to have a relatively good prognosis (Masterson, 1967; Robins, 1978; Rutter, 1972a) and Malmivaara's results are more compatible with a clinic policy of retaining 'neurotic' children for long-term treatment.

SOCIAL AND FAMILY DATA

Various items referred to the child's social and family environment. These included social class, age of parents, parental employment, parental mental and physical health, parental marital status, and primary caretaker and family size. Though these have been implicated at various times in the genesis of childhood disorder, only maternal occupation showed any difference between the index and the control group as a whole. The other family factors do not therefore seem to contribute directly to an increased risk for adult mental health, though it remains possible that each could determine the character of adult disturbance should it occur for other reasons.

Occupation of mother

Employment of mothers was recorded in terms of full-time or part-time employment, and approximately half of all mothers were not employed outside their own homes. Generally, mothers of girls were more likely to be employed, and mothers of controls more than index cases. However, the biggest difference is when these two are put together, that is 25.4 per cent of mothers of control girls were employed full-time as compared with 9.5 per cent of mothers of index girls (Table 3.3).

Table 3.3. *Employment of mothers*

Employment	Male		Female	
	Index N (%)	Control N (%)	Index N (%)	Control N (%)
Housewife	55 (*56.1*)	46 (*46.9*)	31 (*49.2*)	27 (*42.9*)
Part-time	8 (*8.2*)	14 (*14.3*)	11 (*17.5*)	6 (*9.5*)
Full-time	20 (*20.4*)	19 (*19.4*)	6 (*9.5*)	16 (*25.4*)

Male: Index/control χ^2 2.37, d.f.2, NS.
Female: Index/control χ^2 6.28, d.f.2, $p < 0.05$.
Figures show only those where a mother was present and occupational status was recorded.
Percentages are of all males or females.

It has been proposed that for mothers to work outside the home does not of itself cause children to suffer (Wallston, 1973; Rutter & Madge, 1976; Yudkin & Holme, 1963). These authors agree that the nature and consistency of handling is more important whether or not mother is at home. West (1969) found that children of working mothers were less often rated as showing bad conduct. The findings in this study are consistent with West's, particularly for girls, and many factors may operate to explain this. West (1969) implicated family size, though controlling for it still left a difference in the same direction. Maternal competence might play a large part, particularly when the sex difference is taken into account. Working mothers may indeed be more efficient both in their work and mothering and in turn provide a more efficient model particularly for the same sex children. Such conclusions do not, of course, indicate that employment of mothers outside the home is always beneficial.

SYMPTOMS IN CHILDHOOD

Forty-two symptoms were noted as being present or absent during the childhood history, and these were grouped according to the frequency of occurrence in all 322 child case records examined (Table 3.4). Ten symptoms occurred in under 15 per cent of cases, twenty-three in 15 per cent to 29 per cent, eight in 30 per cent to 44 per cent, and one symptom, anxiety, in over 45 per cent of all cases. Though nearly all symptoms appeared more often in the index group, the differences were small and for the whole index group only five reached levels of statistical significance; these included obsessions, sleep disturbance, enuresis, tempers, and peer isolation. When the groups are divided by age and sex further differences are more apparent (Table 3.4). Of the most frequently occurring symptoms two were significantly more common in index children; tempers and peer isolation. For tempers the difference is mainly from all children below the age of 12 and for peer isolation for boys aged under 12. The majority of symptoms fell into the middle frequency group but again only two showed index control differences for the whole group, sleep disturbances and enuresis (the latter more commonly in controls).

When divided by age and sex, aggression or violence and somatic complaints were more common in index boys and poor concentration and over-dependence in younger index boys. In the group of symptoms occurring least commonly, only obsessions were significantly more common in index cases. Some of the individual symptoms are referred to later in the chapters on particular types of disorder, but two symptoms merit further note here, largely because in spite of the overall differences they do not appear linked with any of the particular types of disorder later discussed.

Table 3.4. *Index/control differences in symptoms; subgroups by age and sex*

	N	Index (%)	Controls (%)	
All children	161			
Obsessions		15.5	6.2	**
All children over 12	60			
Sleep disturbance		47.5	15.4	**
All children under 12	101			
Tempers		53.9	36.2	*
Enuresis		22.6	37.3	*
All boys	98			
Aggression/Violence		37.8	24.5	*
Somatic complaints		31.0	18.4	*
Anxiety		49.0	36.7	*
Boys under 12	71			
Peer isolation		43.7	27.8	*
Poor concentration		47.9	29.2	*
Over dependency		32.4	16.7	*

χ^2 *$p < 0.05$, **$p < 0.01$.

Sleep disturbance

Sleep disturbance occurred in just over one third of index cases and in a quarter of controls. For children over the age of 12 the proportion in index cases rises to almost half. There is little difference according to sex, which makes it less likely to be due to a greater incidence of depression in older girls. Though many authors agree on the importance of sleep disturbance, a pattern of association is hard to pin down. Macfarlane and colleagues (1954) found sleep disturbance to be commoner in older and younger children, with a trough in between, but Shepherd and colleagues (1971) could find no age association. The symptom does appear to lead to referral to psychiatric services (Douglas, 1966; Rutter *et al.*, 1970) though Douglas did not report outcome, and Rutter found that the high incidence obscured any specific associations. Though the usual association is with depressive disorders, at least in adults, Robins (1966) did find that it was commoner in children with antisocial behaviour. Two retrospective studies pointed to a link between childhood sleep disorder and adult psychiatric illness in general (Kupfer *et al.*, 1975; Abe, 1972). Abe (1972) made a particular point that sleep disturbance as a symptom tended to have constancy over time for his phobic and nervous mothers. A reminder of the importance of this symptom comes from Thomas (1971). She looked for predictors of potential suicide and found sleep disturbance to be one of the most useful items in a discriminant function analysis, and of more value than depressed feelings.

Apart from the findings of an overall higher incidence in the index group, sleep disturbance showed few clear associations in this study and in a way this is in keeping with the rather varied picture from other studies. None the less, with the finding here it would seem to be a symptom to take seriously and perhaps merits more detailed longitudinal research.

Enuresis

Enuresis was found to occur significantly more often in child controls (29.2 per cent) than in index cases (15.6 per cent). This pattern was similar for boys and girls, though the rates were higher for index and control boys (22.4 per cent and 34.7 per cent) than for index and control girls (12.7 per cent and 20.6 per cent). These rates are in line with other published figures for clinic rates (Shepherd *et al.*, 1971; Douglas & Mulligan, 1961). Shepherd gives a clinic rate of between 12 per cent and 24 per cent, with a moderate predominance in boys.

With regard to the association between enuresis and emotional disorder the literature has given conflicting views. Some attach little significance (Macfarlane *et al.*, 1954; Lapouse & Monk, 1958) whereas others have stressed a link with psychiatric disorder (Michaels, 1955; Stein & Susser, 1966; Sacks, 1974). Rutter and colleagues (1970, 1973) found that rates of deviance were higher in enuretic children, and indeed in this study all children (index and control) had other symptoms present. No particular associations were found within the index group, and the higher rate in control would suggest that the links are with disorder of a good prognosis, perhaps arising from the enuresis rather than causing it.

PERSONALITY DESCRIPTION IN CHILDREN

Various studies have commented on the relevance of childhood personality traits or temperamental characteristics for both childhood and adult disorder (Livson & Peskin, 1967; Bronson, 1967; Graham *et al.*, 1973) though usually retrospective data are used (Kupfer *et al.*, 1975). An attempt was made in this study to extract data according to some of the categories used by Livson, but the recording of information concerning temperament was far less consistent than for symptoms or social data.

The items used included the following: shyness, anxiety, moodiness, expressiveness, aggressiveness, irritability, and dependence. Although for all items an 'extreme' was scored more often for index cases, only moodiness in girls reached statistical significance.

It seemed possible that an overall description of the child in terms of personality extremes might be more likely to separate the index from control cases, and a count of extremes was made for each child (Table 3.5). Using the score no difference was found for boys but significantly more girls in the index groups scored five or more extremes.

The assessment of personality traits or temperamental characteristics presents considerable difficulty though scales are being developed for objective measurement (McDevitt & Casey, 1978; Lyon & Plomin, 1981); Lyon and Plomin still found only moderate agreement between ratings of mothers and fathers. In a detailed review of individual differences Rutter (1977b) concluded that there was good evidence to associate certain temperamental attributes with development of disorder, particularly conduct disorder, and he noted the use of temperamental adversity scores which may be roughly comparable with the score used here. Though the data on temperaments were poorly recorded the fact that some differences were found supports the importance of this type of observation.

INTELLIGENCE AND EDUCATIONAL RETARDATION

Intelligence tests were carried out on the majority of the children. Though a few were tested on the Stanford Binet, the Wechsler Intel-

Table 3.5. *Scores for each child on extreme of personality item*

Score of extreme on personality items	Boys		Girls	
	Index	Control	Index	Control
0	9	15	6	8
1	15	16	5	10
2	20	19	13	12
3	18	23	12	21
4	16	11	10	9
5	9	11	10	1
6	8	3	6	2
7	3	0	1	0
Total	98	98	63	63
Mean score for all cases	2.93	2.6	3.2	2.4

Table 3.6. *Mean score on intelligence tests*

	Index	Control
Number measured	151	155
Mean IQ	97.7	98.7
S.D.	16.3	16.0

ligence Scale for Children (WISC) was used in most cases. Table 3.6 shows the number measured, the mean IQ, and the standard deviation.

Children with an IQ of 60 or less were specifically excluded from the study, so that the distribution must show an abrupt cut-off for the lower range. The means for each group are almost identical, there being no statistical differences, and though for girls there was a small peak in the range 76 to 85 the distribution was remarkably normal. Other studies suggest a relationship between IQ and the incidence of behaviour disorders (Rutter, 1964), but whether specific forms of disorder are associated with low IQ is less clear. Robins (1966) did find that more future sociopaths had an IQ of less than 100, but the results were not statistically significant, an almost identical picture to the findings in this study. Perhaps the greatest relevance of the result here is that other index control differences cannot be attributed to differences in intelligence.

EDUCATIONAL RETARDATION

Educational attainment was measured by various means as part of the psychological testing in many children, though, for the most part, these were tests of reading ability. As the case records were spread over a number of years the nature of the tests used varied and what is recorded here is only whether or not the child was more than one year behind that expected for chronological age on some standardized measure (Table 3.7).

The results indicate that educational retardation was more likely to occur in the index boys, as compared with controls or index girls. Fewer index girls were assessed, but even if all the missing index girls showed educational retardation, the sex differences would remain. The association between educational retardation and childhood disorder has long

Table 3.7. *Educational retardation of more than one year behind chronological age*

	Index	Control	χ^2
Boys $N=98$	71.0 *(80.6)*	41.8 *(80.6)*	$p<0.001$
Girls $N=63$	26.0 *(73.0)*	41.5 *(84.1)*	NS

Figures shown are percentages of those assessed in each group.
Bracketed figures show the percentage of each group total for whom assessment was carried out.

been accepted (Burt, 1925; Rutter, 1970b), and a particular association noted with antisocial behaviour (Glueck & Glueck, 1950; Gibbens, 1963; Rutter, 1970b). Here the link is particularly with those in whom the disorder continues into adult life. These associations are further discussed in Chapter 8 on conduct disorder.

DIAGNOSTIC CATEGORIES

The diagnostic categories used in the study for childhood disorder were derived from the WHO classification of psychiatric disorders in childhood (Rutter *et al.*, 1969). The 15 categories used and definitions are given in Appendix II. The figures are remarkably similar for index cases and controls, with no significant differences (see Tables 1 & 2, Appendix III). In view of this, two other methods of separating the index cases from controls were explored: these were symptom scores and discriminant function analysis.

SYMPTOM SCORES

As noted on many items there were small excesses of index cases scoring positively compared with controls. A number of studies have used symptom scores as a measure of current disturbance (e.g. Glidewell *et al.*, 1957; Shepherd *et al.*, 1971; Rutter *et al.*, 1970) and have found correlation with other criteria such as parent or teacher ratings. It seemed possible therefore that apart from the nature of symptoms or the diagnosis, the actual number of symptoms could relate to prognosis. The number of symptoms recorded positively for each child was totalled to give a straight 'score'. Graph 3.1 shows the distribution of the scores divided into high and low scoring groups.

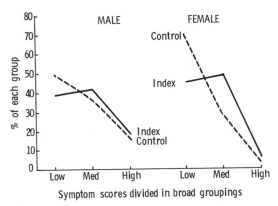

Graph 3.1. Symptom scores divided in broad groupings.

There was no clear 'break point' separating index from controls though some differences were seen. Generally more boys had high scores than girls and index cases than controls. Only two girls in the control group had very high scores and unfortunately only direct follow-up could reveal whether this is meaningful in terms of prognosis. From the results here high scores related to recurrence in adult life but the differences are too small to make the score of assistance in prognosis.

DISCRIMINANT FUNCTION ANALYSIS

Various items showed differences between the index and control group in childhood and though there is good reason to suppose an overlap between the two groups it is possible that using some of the criteria discrimination could be made. On the first 80 cases discriminant function analysis using twenty-four items (see Table A3, Appendix III) had shown significant separation between index and control groups (Zeitlin, 1971) and using the same items the analysis was repeated for all cases,

Table 3.8. *Values for* F *distribution on discriminant function analysis*

All cases	All items	$F(24, 279) = 1.65714, p < 0.05$
Male	All items	$F(24, 171) = 2.15204, p < 0.01$
Male	Selected items	$F(10, 185) = 2.78016, p < 0.01$
Female	All items	$F(24, 101) = 1.49663, NS$
Female	Selected items	$F(11, 114) = 1.96931, p < 0.05$

and for male and female separately. Table 3.8 shows the F distribution for the various analyses.

For all cases the result is significant at the 5 per cent level and using selected items the analysis shows significant separation of the groups when divided accordingly by sex. The main point of these results is that in spite of the relatively small symptomatic and diagnostic differences, the presence of identifiable difference is supported between at least some children destined to have adult illness and those with a good prognosis.

SUMMARY AND CONCLUSION

This section has examined some of the ways in which the index cases differed from the child controls attending the same clinic. In terms of specific items, there is remarkably little difference. Diagnosis helped little and only a few symptoms showed significant difference. The importance of some of these symptoms is discussed later in the relevant chapters. In spite of the lack of clear distinctions of this nature there were differences between the index group and controls that are best seen in terms of a general impression rather than of more formal items. The index cases seemed to be just that much 'worse' than the controls; they attended for longer, had a few more symptoms, a few more adverse character traits, and more educational retardation. This impression was borne out both by that gained from reading the case notes and by the discriminant function tests. Whether these differences apply to the whole group to a greater or lesser extent or particularly to children with some types of disturbance is less clear, though the discriminant function analysis would indicate that it is not solely due to a few very different children. The importance of longitudinal studies is stressed by the findings that the poor outcome was not expected by the contemporary psychiatrist.

4. Adult psychiatric patients with preceding childhood disorder: comparison with adult controls

INDEX CASES AS ADULTS

Both the index and control groups consisted of patients attending the adult departments of the same hospital, the only difference in the selection criteria being absence of any history of childhood disturbance in the control group. The selection did pose some problems. For many the only information was from the patient and rejection of all those without an independent informant would almost certainly have produced a bias in the nature of the disorders present. Any case records with a history of psychiatric assessment or treatment, or any major psychiatric symptoms in childhood were rejected, though care had to be taken not to exclude any merely because of an adverse environment in childhood. The greatest difficulty was with regard to the time of onset of the symptoms present in adult life and the likelihood of deficient reporting of childhood symptoms by the 'adult' patients. This perhaps applied most to those with symptoms suggesting personality disorder. Even though theoretically it is probable that such disorder commenced in childhood, exclusion on these grounds alone would prejudice the issue in a circular fashion, thereby proving that all adults with personality disorder showed overt childhood problems. The standard of case-note recording was actually high and cases rejected as controls for inadequate information did not, at least generally, appear to differ from those selected.

DIAGNOSTIC CATEGORIES

Adults were allocated diagnoses from two scales, the first for clinical syndromes, or specific disorders and the second for personality disorders. For the purpose of comparison, the categories were divided into broad groups of psychosis, non-depressive neurosis, depressive neurosis and personality disorder only.

From Table 4.1 it can be seen that there are relatively few differences and that these mainly apply to women. If all neurotic disorders are taken together it appears that on the whole they are more likely to occur in the control group, but the separation of depressive disorders and obsessional

Table 4.1. *Broad diagnostic grouping for adults*

	Male		Female	
	Index (*N*=98)	Control (*N*=98)	Index (*N*=63)	Control (*N*=63)
Psychosis	14.3	17.4	12.7	11.1
Non-depressive neurosis	14.3	16.4	27.0	12.7
Depressive neurosis	26.6	33.6	38.0	65.0
Others	5.1	0	3.2	4.8
Personality disorder only	39.7	32.6	19.1	6.4

Males χ^2 1.81 d.f.3, NS.
Females χ^2 11.75 d.f.3, $p < 0.01$.
Figures shown are percentage column totals.

disorder shows a slightly different picture (Table 4.2), with non-depressive neurosis being significantly more common in index women. Depressive neurosis occurred more often in controls, the difference for women being considerable. Obsessional disorders show an excess in index males and whilst the difference is small it will be seen subsequently that the index control difference is amplified when the symptom of obsession is considered. Depressive disorders are dealt with further in Chapter 6 and obsessional disorders in Chapter 7.

Personality disorder occurred more often in the male and female index cases though the difference is not as great as might have been expected. Personality disorder also is dealt with in more detail subsequently (Chapter 8) where it will be seen that there are differences, more in severity of the personality disorder, between the index and control

Table 4.2. *Neurotic disorders in index cases and adult controls*

	Male		Female	
	Index (*N*=98)	Control (*N*=98)	Index (*N*=63)	Control (*N*=63)
All forms of neurotic disorders	40.9	50.1	65.1	77.7
Depressive	26.5	33.7	38.1	65.1*
Obsessional	5.1	3.1	7.9	1.6 ⎤*
Other neurosis	9.2	13.3	19.1	11.1 ⎦
All other disorders	39.2	50.0	34.9	22.2

Figures shown are percentages of each column total.
*χ^2 $p < 0.05$ or better.

groups. In examining the incidence of the diagnostic groupings as between the index and control cases it is useful to consider theoretically what might produce a difference. First, it matters whether the grouping does represent a clinical entity. If the grouped symptoms used in forming a diagnosis are completely non-specific, then apart from the effect of the different incidence of individual symptoms, it would be difficult to construct any model to result in a different incidence for those with or without a childhood history. If the diagnoses represent some form of clinical entity then in certain circumstances differences may be apparent. The clearest would be a disorder which was constantly or predominantly manifest in childhood if it appeared in adult life. A second circumstance would be where childhood disorder generally increased the likelihood of a given adult disorder; similarly, the presence of some form of disability predisposing both to childhood disorder and to a specific adult disorder should also be apparent as an incidence differing in the two groups. It is harder to envisage any mechanism that would result in the under-representation of a diagnosis in the index group unless it is proposed that childhood disorder is in some way protective. However, if any conditions occur less frequently in the control group, then with a fixed group size the difference must be 'made up' by an apparent excess of something else. It seems likely that some of the excess of depression in controls is accounted for in this manner.

SYMPTOMS IN ADULT LIFE

At a symptom level there were again few differences. Table 4.3 sum-marizes those that were found. The first four items appeared more commonly in index cases in both males and females. Antisocial behaviour and violence were found more often in index men, and phobias, panic attacks, and tempers were common in index women, though not all of the differences were statistically significant. Five items, all relating to anxiety and depression, were more common in the adult control group.

The results for individual symptoms are consistent with the findings for diagnostic groups. To a large extent the symptoms found more often in index cases relate to personality disorder of some form and those more common in controls to depression. As controls were less likely to show personality disorder it was possible that the higher rates for depressive symptoms were merely an artefact resulting from this. However, differences in the same direction were still present when only those cases without personality disorder were compared.

An impression was gained that in spite of the small differences in symptoms and diagnosis, the controls were generally more 'intact' in their

Table 4.3. *Symptom frequency differences between index cases and adult control groups*

	Male		Female	
	Index (N=98)	Control (N=98)	Index (N=63)	Control (N=63)
A. *Items more frequent in Index Cases*				
Dependency	30.6	15.3**	38.1	17.5**
Obsessions	17.3	7.1*	22.2	9.5*
Poor psycho-sexual adjustment	63.3	53.3	61.9	52.4
Motor disturbance	10.2	4.1	12.7	6.0
Antisocial behaviour	46.9	27.6**	7.9	9.5
Phobias	8.2	7.1	28.6	15.9
Panic attacks	4.1	6.1	12.7	1.6*
Tempers	22.4	22.4	30.2	17.5
B. *Items more frequent in Controls*				
Depression	51.0	69.4**	76.2	87.3
Weight disturbance	5.1	13.3*	22.2	33.3
Lack of confidence	21.4	34.7*	12.7	34.9*
Apathy	24.5	20.4	14.3	30.2*
Anxiety	55.1	68.4	73.0	74.6

Figures shown are percentages of column tables.
χ^2 *$p<0.05$, **$p<0.005$.

functionings and items relating to social competence and success, reflect this.

MARITAL STATUS AND DEPENDENCE

These two items are to some extent linked and therefore are considered together. Table 4.4 shows that for both male and female subjects more index patients were still with their parents, though the reasons appear to differ for men and women. For men, approximately the same number of index and control cases were living alone and the main difference is in the category 'other'. This includes those married and independent, but also those in special hostels, etc. For women, only four index cases were living alone.

Table 4.5 shows the percentage firstly of those ever married, then as a proportion of those ever married the numbers divorced or separated. For women there were no significant differences between index and control cases, about half of all women had been married. Those with personality disorder were more likely to be divorced than those without, but this

Table 4.4. *Dependence in index cases and adult controls*

	Male		Female	
	Index (N=98)	Control (N=98)	Index (N=63)	Control (N=63)
Living with parents	57.1	38.8	44.4	22.2
Living alone	20.4	19.4	6.3	17.5
Other	22.5	41.8	49.3	60.3

Figures shown are percentages of column totals.
Male index/control χ^2 9.2 d.f.2 $p<0.05$.
Female index/control χ^2 8.96 d.f.2 $p<0.05$.

Table 4.5. *Marital status of index cases and adult controls*

	No P.D.		P.D.	
	Index	Control	Index	Control
Males	(N=25)	(N=33)	(N=73)	(N=65)
Ever married	16.0	42.4	27.4	33.9
	(N=4)	(N=14)	(N=20)	(N=22)
Divorced or separated	25.0	7.1	45.0	22.7
Females	(N=23)	(N=39)	(N=40)	(N=24)
Ever married	47.8	64.1	57.5	41.7
	(N=11)	(N=25)	(N=23)	(N=10)
Divorced or separated	9.1	16.0	26.1	40.0

Figures shown are percentages of bracketed totals given above each.
Figures for divorce or separation are of total ever married.
For all males unmarried/married/divorced/separated:
Index/control χ^2 7.88, d.f.2, $p<0.05$.

applied to index and controls alike. For men the pattern is clearer. Fewer index men ever married but of those who did more were divorced or separated compared with control men. Though there were differences between those with and without personality disorder the pattern was the same for all. Of the whole group, 42 per cent of index cases who married were divorced or separated, as compared with only 16.7 per cent of controls.

Note was made of the numbers who cohabited irrespective of marital status and the figures for this tally closely with those for marital status. Only 20 per cent of index men cohabited, as compared with 35.7 per cent of control men and 50.8 per cent of index and control women.

SOCIAL CLASS

Social class was rated according to the HMSO classification of occupations. This classifies occupations largely on the basis of skill and authority so that it affords some degree of rating of success or competence, as the groups were age-matched. Table 4.6 shows the percentage falling into each social category.

Table 4.6. *Social grouping of index cases as adults, compared with adult controls*

	Male		Female	
Social class	Index (N=98)	Control (N=98)	Index (N=63)	Control (N=63)
I and II	5.1	6.1	4.8	20.6
IIIa (non-manual)	13.3	25.5	39.7	36.5
IIIb (manual)	19.4	25.5	19.0	20.6
IV (semi-skilled)	19.4	13.3	19.0	9.5
V (unskilled)	27.6	17.3	11.1	6.3
Student	4.1	8.1	3.2	0
Unemployed	10.2	3.1	3.2	6.3
Not known	1.0	1.0	0	0

Figures shown are percentages of column totals.
Groups I, II and III vs. IV and V (i.e., skilled vs. other).
Male χ^2 7.2 d.f.1, $p < 0.01$.
Female χ^2 3.7 d.f.1 NS.

The index cases, particularly males, were less likely to be in social classes I, II, or III, that is, skilled and professional groups. Re-analysis according to personality disorder showed the difference to persist irrespective of the presence or absence of personality disorder (see Chapter 8). It would seem therefore that overall index cases as a group showed less competence as compared with controls with regard to employment.

Social class difference is of particular importance, first because the comparison is with other patients with more or less the same diagnoses, and secondly because in childhood the social class of the parental family did not differ between index and child control cases. This is emphasized when comparison is made between the social class of index cases as adults and their own parental family.

Of the 161 cases either parental or subject's social class was unknown for three subjects. A further seven were excluded because the status was given as 'student', leaving a total of 151 (see Table A4, Appendix III). The percentage of parents in social class I and II was 10.6, but of the patients whose parents were in these groups 75 per cent were, as adults, in a lower group or unemployed. Social class III (here taking manual and non-manual skilled together) included 51.6 per cent of parents, and of the 78 whose parents were in this social class 43.5 per cent were in a lower group or unemployed, and only 5.8 per cent were in a higher group. Finally, 35.2 per cent of parents were in social classes IV and V and none was unemployed, as compared with 46.7 per cent of index cases in social class IV and V or unemployed. Nineteen (33.4 per cent) whose parents were in this group did, however, rise to a higher social class.

Overall, when the groups are compared between social classes I, II, and III, and IV, V, and Unemployed, significantly more index patients were in lower social classes, as compared with their parental family ($p < 0.05$).

OTHER MARKERS OF IMPAIRMENT

Two further items also indicated that the index group were more impaired and less effective than the adult controls. First, they more often had a court record. 46.9 per cent of males and 11.1 per cent of females attended court for other than civil actions, as compared with 29.6 per cent and 6.3 per cent for controls. The differences in court record were not merely a reflection of the rates of personality disorder, as fewer controls with personality disorder had court records, as compared with index cases receiving the same diagnosis. Further details on antisocial behaviour are given in Chapter 8.

Secondly, about one-quarter of index cases also had major physical disorder, this being twice as often as the controls. Information about the physical disorder varied greatly in the case notes so that no analysis according to physical diagnosis could be made, but neurological disorders, including epilepsy, appeared to feature more than other types of illness.

DISCUSSION

The index cases differed from adult controls only very little on the criteria of symptom and diagnosis. The more striking differences involve factors concerning their personal competence, including marital status, dependence, social class, and physical disorder.

The relatively small phenomenological and syndromal differences are to some extent only to be expected as there are a relatively limited number of ways in which disorder can be manifest. An evaluation of disorder based predominantly on here and now manifestations would tend to produce a similar picture irrespective of the course of events over time.

The main difference would be for symptoms that usually took their origins early in life, and the difference in incidence between obsessions and depression illustrate this. Obsessional disorders are more likely to have commenced in childhood and therefore are overrepresented in the index group. Depression on the other hand appears to be a condition in which the majority do not have childhood antecedents and therefore this tends to be overrepresented in the controls. However, rather than there being specific phenomenological differences the index cases as a whole appeared to be less able when compared with the controls with the same diagnostic labels.

Male index patients were less likely than controls to have married or cohabited and if married were more often divorced. This held true for those with and without personality disorder. Differences were smaller for women in spite of generally higher rates for marriage. Robins (1966) found that a sociopathic group were no less likely to have married, but 51 per cent of men and 70 per cent of women were divorced at least once, as compared with 16 per cent of male and 42 per cent of female controls. She also found an overall divorce rate of 30 per cent for non-sociopathic patients. Robins's results relate more to the effects of socio-pathic personality, whereas the results here apply to all patients, but if personality disorder in this study equated with the sociopathic disorders in Robins's work then the findings are remarkably similar.

Social class differences were present both for men and women and index cases tended to be in lower social classes than either their parental family or patients from the same clinic. Almost 60 per cent of index cases were in unskilled occupation or unemployed. Robins (1966) found that the sociopathic group were also more often in unskilled employment or unemployed, but though the index group here contained a higher proportion with personality disorder, (compared with controls), the overall pattern was still present when all cases with personality disorder were excluded. Birtchnell (1971) noted a general tendency for a downward social drift in psychiatric patients except for those with neurosis, but as the controls here are also psychiatric patients and the proportions with neurotic disorder are very similar, the 'patient status' alone cannot account for the social class differences.

A minority of index and control patients suffered from serious or chronic physical disorder, but almost twice as many index cases were so affected. Some of the work on the effects of significant life events indicates that physical illness is a contributory factor to the genesis of psychiatric disorder (Myers *et al.*, 1972). Since both groups in this study are psychiatric patients, again it is difficult to explain the raised incidence in those who were disturbed in childhood except for the possibility of chronic physical illness as an aetiological factor both in childhood and adult life. The case notes did not consistently give details of the nature of physical problems but the general impression was of a greater frequency of organic neurological disorder. Gibbens (1963) found that 22 per cent of delinquent adolescents had a history of minor physical illness and 18 per cent had had severe illness as compared with 11 per cent and 4 per cent of controls. He suggested three possible mechanisms for the association: 1. direct, as a results of brain injury or encephalitis; 2. economic, i.e., the difficulty of earning a living; and 3. psychological reaction to illness. There is no reason why all three should not operate together and it seems apparent that, at least for some individuals, physical disorder commencing early in life and persisting may also have far greater impact on psychological development than is at first apparent.

5. Symptomatic and diagnostic continuities from childhood to adult life

Chapters 3 and 4 have shown that differences do exist between the index cases and both control groups, though generally in symptoms and diagnosis they are quite similar. In this chapter a general look is taken at the index group for continuities between childhood and adult life, and subsequent chapters, 6 to 9, deal with specific types of disorder in more detail.

SYMPTOM CONTINUITY

The same or similar terms were used for some items in the adult records as were used in the child records and this was reflected in the symptom lists. The data were examined to see whether those children who showed a given symptom showed it again as an adult. From Table 5.1 it can be seen that all of the symptoms occurred more frequently if they had

Table 5.1. *Symptoms described in adult life and childhood by the same term*

	Proportion of children going on to show relevant symptom during adult attendance		
	Absent in childhood	Present in childhood	Significance on χ^2 test
Obsessions	9.6	72.0	$p < 0.001$
Aggression/violence	14.3	38.1	$p < 0.01$
Depression	43.5	85.0	$p < 0.001$
Phobias	7.3	42.1	$p < 0.001$
Headaches	8.5	52.7	$p < 0.001$
Somatic complaints	17.4	38.5	$p < 0.01$
Attention seeking	3.7	33.3	$p < 0.001$
Anxiety	48.6	73.5	$p < 0.01$
Tempers	10.5	33.3	$p < 0.025$
Difficult at school/Work failure	37.9	55.5	NS
Dependence	21.2	42.0	NS
Lack of confidence	10.9	23.8	NS

already appeared in childhood, and for most the association was statistically significant.

The association between the presence of obsessions as a symptom in childhood and in adult life was one of the strongest found. Obsessions are usually regarded as an uncommon symptom but here 38 of the 161 index cases (23.6 per cent) showed the symptom at some point in their psychiatric records, and of these 65.8 per cent had presented in childhood. Because of the prominence of this symptom within the index group obsessional disorders are examined in more detail in a separate chapter (see Chapter 7).

Phobias also showed clear evidence of continuity but, though very few without the symptom in childhood showed it in adult life for the first time, under half (42.1 per cent) of those with the childhood symptom continued with it during their adult illness. This contrasts with the 72 per cent of 'repeat' for obsessions. Of the 16 subjects with continuity of phobias 11 also showed obsessions at some points, perhaps indicating a special 'bad' prognosis when both are present.

The continuity for aggressive behaviour applied mainly to boys and for males only 40.5 per cent of those aggressive as children were again so in adult life, as compared with 18.0 per cent of non-aggressive boys. Violent and aggressive behaviour also showed an important correlation with adult diagnosis. Of the 42 children said to show such behaviour 37 were later diagnosed as having personality disorder and the remaining five were all said to show psychosis (Table 5.2).

Table 5.2. *Childhood aggression and adult diagnosis*

| | Personality disorder | | | |
| | Male P.D. | | Female P.D. | |
Aggression in childhood	Absent	Present	Absent	Present
Absent	23	38 (62.3%)	22	36
Present	3*	34 (91.9%)	2*	3

*=adult psychosis.
For males χ^2 8.89 d.f.1, $p < 0.05$.

A comparison of those with continuity of aggressive behaviour and those without gives some additional information. On most items the two groups were identical, but Table 5.3 shows some differences. Those showing aggressive behaviour for the first time in adult life tended to be brighter and to show more disability in some form. Four had epilepsy,

Table 5.3. *Comparison of index cases with continuity of aggression and those with aggression only in adult life*

	Aggression only as adult (*N*=16)	Aggression as adult and child (*N*=16)
Mean age at childhood presentation	11.75	9.9
Mean IQ as child*	100.6	92.3
Sex ratio M:F	22.1	15.1
Neurological abnormality	7	0
Developmental delay or chronic physical disorder	11	7

The last two rows overlap.
*Test just fails to reach 5 per cent level.

one had chorea, one had brain damage, (clumsiness, verbal-performance IQ difference, abnormal EEG), and one had spasms involving the head.

Six subjects showed no aggressive or other antisocial behaviour in childhood but none the less went on to show aggressive behaviour in adult life. The brief notes below show some of the diversity of symptoms shown, and though psychosis and neurological damage seemed related to some of these exceptions it did not account for all.

Case 5809 Male	Childhood: school refusal.
	Adult: alcoholism, aggression, failure to maintain job.
Case 5103 Male	Childhood: obsessions, temper tantrums.
	Adult: aggressive outbursts, obsessions, sexual deviance.
Case 5502 Male	Childhood: disobedience, fears, obsessions, isolated.
	Adult: schizophrenia, aggressive.
Case 5803 Male	Childhood: anxiety, stomach aches, depression, sleep disturbance, delusions, hallucinations, incongruous behaviour, polio.
	Age 5, diagnosis: psychosis.
	Adult: antisocial behaviour, homeless, jobless, friendless, physical symptoms, depressed, violent, prison record.
Case 5504 Female	Childhood: clumsy, verbal/performance IQ difference, fidgety, developmental delay.
	Adult: overactive, violent.
Case 5404 Female	Childhood: hysteria, screaming fits, fears, pulmonary tuberculosis.
	Adult: obsessions, aggression, depressed.

For all cases quoted in the text brief summaries are given in Appendix I.

OTHER SYMPTOMS

The other symptoms shown in Table 5.1 were further analysed for differences according to age, sex, and the presence of personality disorder. In all subgroups the correlations between occurrence of a symptom in childhood and adult life persisted. Though the antisocial behaviours were fairly specific to the groups showing personality disorder, other symptoms were distributed through all diagnostic groups and the continuity of symptoms appeared to be independent of diagnosis.

DIAGNOSTIC CONTINUITIES

Care was taken to ensure that knowledge of the childhood data did not influence research assessment of the adult data and vice versa; this being particularly important for diagnostic rating. It was hoped therefore that diagnostic continuities would be valid and shed some light on the usefulness of childhood categories as indicators of prognosis. Tables 5.4a and b show the cross tabulation for the broader diagnostic groups. In these tables personality disorder refers to those cases where no other diagnosis was given. A further analysis was made according to all cases with personality disorder, irrespective of other psychiatric syndromes present (Table 5.5). Whilst diagnostic continuity was not as clear as symptom continuity several particular aspects are worth further note.

Psychosis Psychosis, if identified in childhood, has a high probability of being diagnosed again in adult life. Of the ten children with this diagnosis, nine were again said to be psychotic as adults, and the tenth was the subject of considerable debate between psychosis and personality disorder. Psychotic disorders are considered in greater detail in Chapter 9.

Emotional—neurotic continuity When all forms of emotional disorder are considered there were 29 boys and 31 girls, of whom 75 per cent went on to show some form of adult neurotic disorder, if reactive depression is included. Of these 60 cases some had other disorders also present in childhood, including conduct disorder. Ten boys and twenty girls were given a diagnosis of emotional disorder only and for this pure group over 83 per cent went on to some form of adult neurotic disorder. Though the continuity from emotional disorder in childhood to neurotic disorder in adult life was strongest for those with no other childhood diagnosis, the coexistence of other types of disorder only slightly reduced the link.

Robins (1966, 1978) proposed that childhood antisocial behaviour was always present if the outcome in adult life included antisocial

Table 5.4. *Childhood and adult diagnosis in broad groupings*

Childhood diagnosis	Adult diagnosis											Total
	Psychosis		Depression		Other neurosis		P.D.		Other		
	(N)	(%)	(N)	(%)	(N)	(%)	(N)	(%)	(N)	(%)	
(a) *Male*											
Psychosis	3	75.0	0	0	0	0	1	25.0	0	0	4
Emotional disorder	2	6.9	9	31.0	9	31.0	8	27.6	1	3.5	29
Conduct & delinquency	6	14.0	11	25.6	2	4.7	24	55.8	0	0	43
Mixed conduct and emotional	2	8.3	8	33.3	4	16.7	7	29.2	3	12.5	24
Developmental disorder	8	28.6	4	14.3	1	3.6	13	46.4	2	7.1	28
Enuresis	0	0	4	36.4	1	9.9	4	36.4	2	18.2	11
(b) *Female*											
Psychosis	6	100	0	0	0	0	0	0	0	0	6
Emotional disorder	0	0	11	35.5	16	51.6	4	12.9	0	0	31
Conduct & delinquency	2	13.3	7	46.7	1	6.7	4	26.7	1	0	15
Mixed conduct and emotional	0	0	6	75.0	0	0	2	25.0	0	0	8
Developmental disorder	0	0	1	20.0	0	0	3	60.0	1	0	5
Enuresis/Encopresis	1	14.3	3	42.9	0	0	2	28.7	1	0	7

Table shows only major diagnostic groups.
Percentages shown are of childhood subcategory.
P.D. = Personality disorder and no other diagnosis.

Table 5.5. *Correlation of childhood diagnoses with all adult personality disorder (irrespective of other psychiatric syndromes)*

Childhood diagnosis	Male		Female	
	N	P.D. present %	*N*	P.D. present %
Psychosis	4	25.0	6	0
Emotional disorder	29	69.0	31	61
Conduct disorder and delinquency	43	90.7	15	80
Mixed conduct and emotional	24	66.7	8	87.5
Developmental disorder	28	78.6	5	80.0
Enuresis/encopresis	11	90.9	7	71.4

Percentage figures shown are percentages of *N* given for each childhood subgroup.

behaviour. Here 11 boys appeared to show only emotional disorder in childhood, and antisocial or aggressive type of personality disorder in adult life, and this would be very much against Robins's view. The case notes of these 11 were therefore re-examined and for most a continuity for antisocial behaviour from childhood was indeed present. Four showed emotional disorder plus delinquency in childhood, one showed obsessional disorder plus conduct disorder, and three showed violence as a symptom. The remaining three, Cases 5710, 5221, and 5401 were apparently true exceptions. These are presented in more detail in Chapter 8 but some similarity existed for the three. All presented before the age of 13, lived with their natural parents, and showed dependency and an aversion to school.

Viewed from adult life the continuity for neurotic disorder was still apparent but there was an important difference between depressive neurosis and other forms of adult neurotic disorder. This latter group consisted of 14 male and 17 female index cases, and of these only one male and one female had not received a childhood diagnosis of emotional disorder, this continuity being irrespective of the presence of antisocial behaviour. In contrast, 32 per cent of adults with neurotic depression did not receive a childhood diagnosis of emotional disorder. The one male exception, Case 5721, was a dull boy who exposed himself; in adult life he worked as a welder, aspired to be an artist, but suffered from anxiety and panic attacks. The case records revealed, however, that anxiety was also a dominant feature of the childhood picture, and the diagnosis in childhood was determined by the presence of 'exposure' and to some extent by the mother's reluctance to make any complaint 'against' him. The female case 4822 presented in childhood with stealing and a clear picture of conduct disorder; she was said to show anxiety and sleep disturbance but these were not dominant features of the clinical picture. In adult life she complained of anxiety, panic attacks and misery but also had evidence for serious personality difficulties.

Details of further differences between depressive disorders and other neurotic disorders are given in Chapter 6, but though numbers were small it appeared that the non-depressive neuroses group was itself not uniform in terms of childhood antecedent disorders (Table 5.6).

Table 5.6. *Comparison between antecedents of anxiety neurosis, obsessive compulsive neurosis, and other non-depressive neurosis*

| Childhood disorder | Adult disorder | | | | | |
| | Anxiety neurosis | | Obsessive compulsive | | Other non-depressive neurosis | |
	M	F	M	F	M	F
Emotional disorder	3	2	3	5	3	9
Mixed conduct and emotional	2	0	2	0	0	0
Conduct	2	1	0	0	0	0
Delinquency	0	0	0	0	0	0
Total	6*	3	5	5	3	9

(a) *One child with conduct disorder and obsessional neurosis in childhood.
(b) Delinquency is included to demonstrate pattern.

Developmental delay and adult diagnosis Developmental delay of some form was diagnosed in 33 children. Viewed from childhood it is difficult to see the associations with adult disorder, but Table 5.7 shows the percentage of adult diagnostic groups given this childhood diagnosis (irrespective of other aspects of childhood disorder).

From Table 5.7 it can be seen that there are links between childhood developmental disorder and both personality disorder and psychosis, as about one-third of these had received that childhood diagnosis. This is a marked contrast to the adult neurotic group and for non-depressive neurosis only one of 32 cases showed developmental delay.

AGE OF CHILDHOOD PRESENTATION AND ADULT DISORDER

Continuities examined so far concern symptoms and diagnosis, but it is possible to look at the age of childhood presentation irrespective of the

Table 5.7. *Developmental delay and adult diagnosis*

Psychosis (N=22)	Non-depressive neurosis (N=32)	Depressive neurosis (N=50)	Personality disorder (N=32)
36.4	3.2	10.0	31.2

Figures are percentages of N for each column, showing developmental delay. For all groups χ^2 15.73 d.f.3 $p < 0.005$.

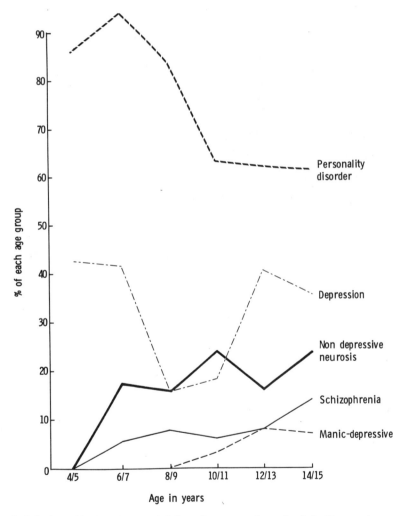

Graph 5.1. Age distribution at childhood presentation of adult diagnostic groups (index cases).

type of symptom. Graph 5.1 shows the proportion of each age group at childhood first presentation who proceeded to a given adult diagnostic group. It can be seen that the different adult disorders present in quite different ways. The commonest adult diagnosis, personality disorder, tended to be less likely as age of first presentation increased, whereas for other diagnoses except depression the reverse is true.

For non-depressive neurosis the slope is almost flat from age 6 to 15. That for schizophrenia rises slowly from 6 to 12 and more steeply to the 14/15 age group, but for manic-depressive psychosis no child presented with anything below the age of 10. The curve for reactive depression shows a very characteristic U shape and it was of note in this study that no matter how the age of childhood onset was examined this pattern persisted.

DISCUSSION

Twelve symptoms demonstrated continuity within the sample examined. Though three just failed to reach levels of statistical significance, the other nine show clearly significant association from childhood to adult life. Various studies have looked at continuities across time though most have concentrated on character traits (Bronson, 1967; Kupfer *et al.*, 1975), or on patterns of behaviour (Carizio, 1968). Abe (1972), in a study ostensibly of children, also obtained retrospective information about the mothers. He found correlation between symptoms in childhood and in adult life in the mothers for headaches, insomnia, and indecision. Other studies have also found continuity for obsessions (see Chapter 7) and for aggression (see Chapter 8). It does seem from this study that, once a symptom occurs in childhood, that symptom will tend to recur if disturbance arises again. It is less clear whether this represents an inbuilt manner of reaction to disturbance or stress, a learned pattern of behaviour, or the constant expression of a disordered mechanism. Anxiety appeared in a relatively large proportion of children, 54 per cent, and recurred in the majority of those, 73.5 per cent. However, it also appeared in almost 50 per cent of adults who had not shown anxiety in childhood. A similar pattern was seen for the symptom of depression though the incidence was lower. This would seem to be a less specific reaction which none the less occurs more readily in some individuals than others. Obsessions, by contrast, appeared in far fewer children, but with a very high likelihood of recurrence. Most other symptoms fell between these two examples.

Marks (1973) noted a lack of evidence about the relationship between phobias in childhood and adult life. In this study significantly more children with phobias showed the same symptom again as adults, as compared with those without the symptom in childhood, and the majority of adults with phobias (61 per cent) had also shown the symptom in childhood. The incidence of phobias was lower than obsessions and comparisons with controls did not indicate any significant difference. It seems from the results here that whilst phobias show symptom continuity they do not carry an increased risk for adult disorder. It should be noted that irrational fears that are not disabling and that fade with time are common in childhood (Shepherd *et al.*, 1966; Marks, 1973) but an attempt was made here to distinguish such fears and not include them as the symptom. That many children with phobias did not have them again in adult life may none the less indicate difficulty in diagnostic distinction. Similarly, the overlap between those with phobias continuing into adult life and the simultaneous presence of obsessions could also represent a difficulty of distinction of phenomena.

Aggression or violent behaviour in childhood showed symptom continuity into adult life but was of particular note because of the strong relationship to adult diagnostic groups. Nearly all violent children showed personality disorder later, and the exceptions showed psychosis. The findings in this study with regard to antisocial behaviour are in accord with those of Robins (1966, 1978) except that she states that "adult antisocial behaviour virtually requires childhood antisocial behaviour". There were exceptions to that rule in this study. Those individuals though were not typical of Robins's sociopathic subjects and organic factors seemed to be more evident.

The continuity of symptoms has implications for nosology. If symptom patterns were representative of discrete entities then diagnostic continuity should compare favourably with individual symptom continuity; that is, individual symptoms might occur in a wide range of disorders which had very different expression in adult life. However, in this study symptom continuity was far more impressive than diagnostic continuity.

Diagnostic continuity was best for psychosis, as virtually all children so diagnosed in the index group again showed a psychotic disorder in adult life (see Chapter 9). The prognosis for early onset psychosis is generally held to be bad. Masterson (1958) found that 58 per cent of adolescents had severe handicap at follow-up 8 to 22 years later, though Eggers (1978) was a little less pessimistic, finding that 20 per cent had complete remission 20 years later.

This study on the whole supports the emotional disorder/conduct disorder distinction (Rutter, 1978), but there are some points worth noting. First, instead of there being a marked distinction, emotional disorder and conduct disorder each showed continuity into adult life more or less independently of the other. This was best seen in comparing pure groups with those with 'mixed' symptomatology. Secondly, depression behaved very differently from other emotional disorders in that it was equally related to conduct disorder and emotional disorder.

The pattern showing age of childhood presentation of various adult disorders is important because it does not require a particular symptom to have been present. The differences between the various adult diagnostic groups is quite striking. The curves for schizophrenia and manic depressive psychosis are to be expected from other studies with a slowly rising incidence for schizophrenia (Eggers, 1978; Rutter, 1978) and an abrupt start in the early teens for manic depressive disorders (Dahl, 1971). The explanation for the curve for personality disorder may be that any disorder presenting early in childhood is grosser and more disabling or that it is more likely to have profound effects on emotional and personality development. Alternatively, children presenting early may be no more disturbed but live in more deviant families. Arguments in favour of each may be found (Gross & Wilson, 1974; Rolf & Garmezy, 1974; Shepherd *et al.*, 1971) but probably all contribute.

6. Depression

The concept of depression is essentially derived from adult psychiatry and the incidence and classification of depressive disorders in adults is still a matter of debate, (Kendell, 1968; Kiloh & Garside, 1963; Rawnsley, 1968; Spicer et al., 1973; Paykel & Rowan, 1979). Depression is, though, one of the commonest diagnoses made in adult life. In childhood misery and tearfulness are also extremely common, but most cannot be construed as being depressed, (Rutter et al., 1970; Graham, 1974, 1981). The nature and classification of depression in children is if anything more problematic than in adults (Cytryn & Mcknew, 1972, 1974; Makita, 1974; Graham, 1981; Kashani et al., 1981) and the identification of links between adult depression and childhood disorder could help clarify a number of issues. So far most studies have searched for environmental antecedents and few have shown clinical associations.

This chapter will consider some indicators of childhood depression, the clinical links with adult depression and other adult disorders and finally other antecedents of adult depression. To start, however, it is necessary to look at the pattern of depressive disorder in the index cases in adult life.

DEPRESSION IN ADULT LIFE

During adult life 51 per cent of male and 76.2 per cent of female index cases complained of depressed mood. For both men and women this was less than in control cases where the figures were 69.4 per cent and 87.3 per cent (Table 6.1). The sex difference was significant for both index and control cases but the difference between index and control cases was relatively small and not statistically significant for women.

The pattern for depression as a diagnosis in adult life was similar to that for the symptom, except that there are fewer in all groups. Again the diagnosis was more likely in women, as compared with men, and in controls, as compared with index cases, both differences being statistically significant at the 1 per cent level or better (Table 6.1).

Neurotic depression was, in fact, the most frequent adult diagnosis made. Comparative figures are difficult to find, as for example in Robins's study (Robins, 1966), where depression was not specifically referred to as an adult diagnosis, though in 18 per cent of sociopathic adults admitted to hospital the reason for admission was given as depression or suicidal attempt. Pritchard and Graham (1966) diagnosed depression in 21 per cent of all cases who had attended also in childhood. Perhaps the best figures for comparison are the Maudsley Triennial statistics (Hare, 1971) where for all out-patients the percentages of men and women with neurotic depression were 15.7 per cent and 35 per cent. These proportions differ significantly from controls used in this study in spite of the fact that they are from the same out-patient depart-

Table 6.1. *Incidence of depression as a symptom and diagnosis in adult life*

	Male (N=98)		Female (N=63)	
	Index	Control	Index	Control
Depression as symptom	51.0	69.4	76.2	87.3
Diagnosis as depression	26.5	33.7	38.1	65.1

Figures shown are percentages of column totals.
All male/female and index/control differences are significant at $p<0.01$ or better, except female index/control for the symptom.

ment. Most other diagnoses were given in roughly similar proportions and the explanation for the difference would seem to lie in two factors. First, the adult age range in this study is restricted to a group in which the incidence of neurotic depression is higher (Spicer *et al.*, 1973). Secondly, the Maudsley statistics give personality disorder as an alternative diagnosis barring the possibility of diagnosing neurotic depression in personality-disordered individuals. When personality disorder is excluded from the Maudsley figures and personality 'disorder only' is excluded from the study figures, then the percentages are 31 per cent and 45 per cent for the former and 40 per cent and 68 per cent for the latter, a much smaller difference than before. In this study depression related to conduct disorder and adult personality disorder in a way that other emotional disorders did not. It seems essential therefore that these are not made to be mutually exclusive. The results actually show that the presence or absence of personality disorder made only a little difference to the incidence of depression in the index cases (Table 6.2). However, taking all factors into account in this study, the control group showed a higher incidence of depressive disorder, and this is in keeping with Rutter's view (Rutter, 1972a) that depression is more likely to start in adult life without childhood antecedents.

Table 6.2. *Depression as symptom and diagnosis in adult life and personality disorder in index cases*

	Male		Female	
	No P.D. (*N*=25)	P.D. (*N*=73)	No P.D. (*N*=23)	P.D. (*N*=4)
Depression as a symptom	68.0	45.2	73.9	77.5
Depression as a diagnosis	28.0	26.0	30.4	42.5

Figures shown are percentages of column totals.
P.D.=personality disorder.

INDICATORS OF CHILDHOOD DEPRESSION

The simplest criterion used for childhood depression was the symptom of depressed mood alone, and this occurred in 28.6 per cent of index cases and 22.4 per cent of the child controls. When divided by age and sex (Table 6.3), there are no clear differences between index and control cases, but a larger proportion of older children complained of the symptom, the difference for girls being significant at the 5 per cent level.

The incidence of the symptom in childhood was plotted according to

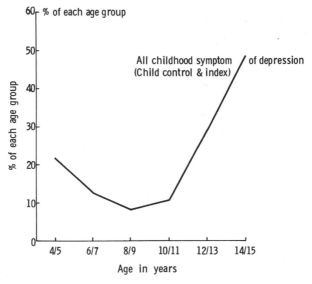

Graph 6.1. Age distribution at first presentation of all children with symptom of depression.

Table 6.3. *Incidence of depression as a symptom in childhood*

	Male		Female	
	Age 0–12 (N=71)	Age 13+ (N=27)	Age 0–12 (N=31)	Age 13+ (N=32)
Symptom of depression				
Index cases	16.9	22.2	22.6	65.6
Control cases	6.3	26.9	15.6	56.3

Figures shown are percentages of each column total.
Female index cases younger vs. older χ^2 10.14, d.f.1, $p<0.005$.
Female control cases younger vs. older χ^2 4.47, d.f.1, $p<0.05$.

age of first presentation and it can be seen that for all 322 children in the study there is a characteristic U-shaped curve, Graphs 6.1, 6.2a and b.

The relationship of the symptom of depression to the various childhood diagnostic categories was also examined and it was apparent that there was no exclusive association. For boys the incidence of depression in the diagnostic groups was fairly uniform, and as many boys with the symptom were allocated a diagnosis of conduct disorder or delinquency as were allocated one of neurotic disorder. For girls a different pattern was noted, in that consistently about 50 per cent of each diagnostic group complained of depression, except for conduct disorder and delinquency where the rate was 13.3 per cent.

A distinction was made during the data abstraction between the symptom with a definite onset and a habitual manner of moodiness. This helped identify the symptom, but the data concerning moodiness was itself too unreliable for further analysis. A search was made for some means of characterizing a syndrome of childhood depression.

Depressive syndromes No formal category of clinical depression was available on the childhood diagnostic scale used, reflecting the difficulties involved in identifying such an entity.

Pearce (1974, 1977) proposed various criteria for a childhood depressive syndrome on the basis of a study of 547 children. He put forward three conditions to define the syndrome; two involved duration of mood change and social and cognitive impact and could not really be matched from the data in this study, but the third depended on the coexistence of various symptoms. Nine of the childhood symptoms recorded in this study seemed to match these. According to Pearce's criteria for the syndrome, depressed mood was required plus at least two other symptoms and such a syndrome was generated with the use of a

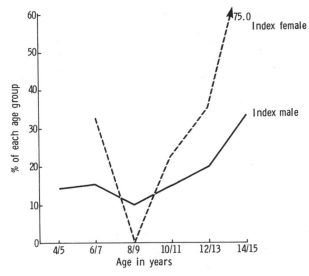

Graph 6.2 (a). Age distribution at first presentation of index children with symptom of depression.

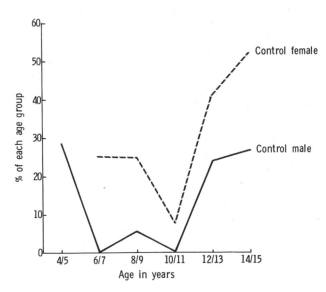

Graph 6.2 (b). Age distribution at first presentation of control chilren with symptom of depression.

computer. The symptoms concerned were: depressed mood, irritability, poor apetite, tempers, obsessions, bodily symptoms, sleep disturbance, fears and peer isolation, and the generated syndrome was designated syndrome X.

Thirteen index males and 24 females showed this syndrome in child-hood and there was virtually no difference between index cases and controls. Graphs 6.3 and 6.4a and b show the age-related distribution,

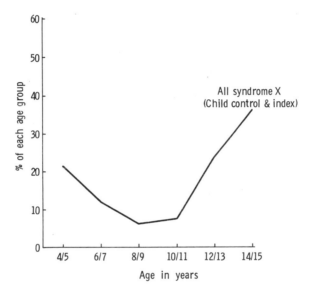

Graph 6.3. Age distribution at first presentation of all children with syndrome X.

and again the very characteristic U-shape of the curves, of childhood depression. The overall rates in the index and control cases were 23 per cent and 18 per cent, only a little lower than for the symptom alone, and the age and sex distribution was almost identical.

Few studies give clear data on the incidence of childhood depression. In this study, on the criteria of the symptom or syndrome X, about 20 per cent of all children showed depression, except for older girls, where the rate was as high as 60 per cent.

Pritchard and Graham (1966) also noted a clinic rate of about 19 per cent but made no division by age and sex. The graph of age of presenta-tion shows that the age-related incidence was far from uniform, but the steep rise after the age of 12 is in keeping with the observations of Rutter (1979) who reported similar findings in the whole population in the follow-up study of children on the Isle of Wight. Kashani and colleagues

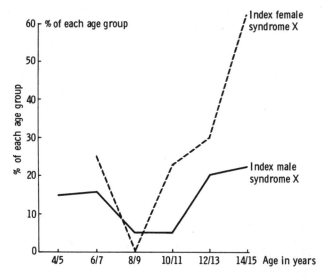

Graph 6.4 (a). Age distribution at first presentation of index children with syndrome X.

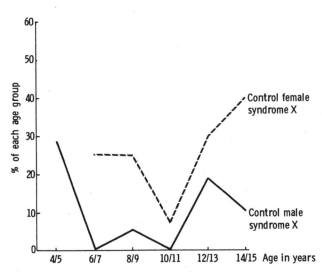

Graph 6.4 (b). Age distribution at first presentation of control children with syndrome X.

(1981) reviewed the prevalence figures for childhood depression and found the following wide variations:

    Whole population   0.14 per cent to 1.9 per cent
    Clinic population   0.8   per cent to 13.7 per cent
    Psychiatric inpatients 23.0 per cent to 59 per cent

The subjects in this study would include both in-patients and out-patients, but none the less show quite a high rate by comparison. The sample was not unusual for age and sex distribution and the most likely explanation is that depression was identified irrespective of any other diagnosis also being given.

The results so far indicate that depression was common in the index cases both in adult life and childhood, but probably most depressed adults had not been depressed as children. However though childhood depression may not increase the probability of adult disorder a different issue is whether there is continuity when both childhood and adult disorder occur, for whatever reason.

CHILD/ADULT CORRELATIONS FOR DEPRESSION

Two different types of correlation between the childhood and adult data referring to depression were considered: first, whether depression or markers of depression in childhood showed constancy with time into adult life, and secondly whether there were any clinical or environmental factors in childhood that were clear antecedents to adult depression in this group.

SYMPTOM AND DIAGNOSTIC CONTINUITY

Adult correlations for the childhood symptom There was strong correlation between the presence of the symptom of depression in childhood and the complaint of depression in adult life; 84.8 per cent of children with the symptom went on to complain of it as an adult as compared with 51.3 per cent of those who had not shown the symptom ($p < 0.0005$) (Table 6.4). Exclusion of those with affective psychosis in adult life does not alter the strength of this link.

Table 6.4 shows the figures for the whole group for clarity, but the association was found to hold true irrespective of sex, the development of personality disorder, or age of presentation in childhood. If anything, the association is stronger for those with personality disorder ($p < 0.01$) than for those without ($p < 0.05$).

The outcome of the childhood symptom with regard to the diagnosis of depression in adult life showed a much weaker association, 46.3 per cent of children with depressed mood were given an adult diagnosis of

Table 6.4. *Outcome for depressed mood in terms of adult depression*

		Adult symptom		Adult diagnosis	
		Absent	Present	Absent	Present
Symptom of depression in childhood	Absent	56	59	82	31
	Present	7	39	22	19

Symptom/symptom χ^2 15.46 d.f.1, $p < 0.0005$.
Symptom/diagnosis χ^2 4.91 d.f.1, $p < 0.05$.

neurotic depression, as compared with 27.4 per cent of non-depressed children ($p < 0.05$). If those with affective psychosis are included, the figures rise a little to 52.5 per cent and 28.7 per cent. The association is slightly stronger for girls than for boys and again the presence of personality disorder made little difference.

Adult correlations for syndrome X Syndrome X related to adult depression in a manner similar to the childhood symptom alone, but the association with the clinical diagnosis was very weak. The figures in Table 6.5 are for the whole group but the association was almost identical for both males and females separately.

The data were further divided according to personality disorder in adult life and syndrome X was found in a smaller proportion of those destined to show personality disorder. This also applied to both male and female and was significant at the 0.5 per cent level. Comparison with the rates for child controls indicated that in this respect the future personality disorder group were similar to the controls, and that there was a relative excess of syndrome X in those without personality disorder.

Table 6.5. *Outcome for childhood syndrome X in terms of adult depression*

		Adult symptom		Adult diagnosis	
		Absent	Present	Absent	Present
Syndrome X	Absent	59	65	90	34
	Present	4	33	21	16

For symptom χ^2 16.18 d.f.1, $p < 0.0005$.
For diagnosis χ^2 N.S.

Syndrome continuity into adult life The childhood syndrome X is a derived syndrome rather than a clinical diagnosis and depends on the presence of specific symptoms. In view of the stability of symptoms over time a similar depressive syndrome designated syndrome Z was derived for adults. This used the same or comparable symptoms in the adult records as did syndrome X from the childhood records.

Thirty-seven children showed syndrome X and of these 31 (83.8 per cent) went on to syndrome Z. This is the strongest link found for any connection between depression in childhood and adult life. Table 6.6 shows the analysis according to sex, and other analyses were carried out according to age and the presence of personality disorder. Though numbers became quite small, the pattern was the same for all groups and, for example, children aged 12 or less showed almost the same proportion going from syndrome X to syndrome Z (80 per cent) as did those over the age of 12 (86 per cent).

Table 6.6. *Association between childhood syndrome X and adult syndrome Z*

| Childhood syndrome X | Adult depressive syndrome Z | | | | | |
| | Male | | | Female | | |
	Absent	Present	Total	Absent	Present	Total
Absent	53	32	85	17	22	39
Present	4	9	13	2	22	24
Total	57	41	98	19	44	63

Male χ^2 4.62, d.f.1, $p < 0.05$.
Female χ^2 8.77, d.f.1, $p < 0.005$.

These results may be taken in conjunction with the rates of the generated syndromes in the control groups. Syndrome X occurred in 23.0 per cent of index cases and 16.8 per cent of controls and syndrome Z in 52.8 per cent of index cases and 57.8 per cent of controls. The index control difference in adults for the clinical diagnosis is almost lost and both syndromes appear in index cases in almost identical number as in controls. One possible explanation is that, unlike the clinical diagnosis, syndrome Z could be identified if the correct symptoms were present no matter what other diagnosis was made.

Masked depression The continuities both for the symptom of depression and the syndromes are very striking in the strength of the association and in the presence in all of the subcategories examined. It is surprising therefore that this has not been found in other studies. One explanation for an apparent lack of continuity has been the concept of masked depression in childhood (Frommer, 1968). While this has tended to fall out of favour, Puig-Antich (Puig-Antich & Gittelman, 1982) still thought it merited further research. There are two ways in which this study can help on this particular point. First, a strong continuity between childhood syndrome X and adult depression having been found, masked depression might be expected to show a similar correlation in the absence of overt depressed mood in childhood. Pearce (1977) commented on this, though he felt that the mood change could always be detected. None the less it is possible that the childhood syndrome could exist in the absence of overt mood change. A second syndrome Y was generated, using the same criteria except that it required not the mandatory presence of depressed mood, but any three of the designated symptoms. Fifty-nine children showed syndrome Y and overall the results are very simlar to those for syndrome X. Though the associations are less strong for syndrome Y the symptom list included depression as a possible symptom and if those with syndrome Y but without the symptom of depression are considered, then the link with adult depression vanishes (Table 6.7).

Table 6.7. *Childhood syndrome Y and adult depression in index cases*

Childhood status	(*N*)	Adult depression as a symptom (%)	Adult depression as a diagnosis (%)
No depressive syndrome	124	52.4	27.4
Syndrome X	37	89.2	43.2
Syndrome Y	22	50.0	27.3

Figures shown are percentages of childhood subgroup total *N*, given for each row, showing depression as adult.
Syndrome Y here refers only to those without depressed mood as a child.

A second way of examining the question of masked depression is to look at the childhood symptoms of adults with depression. A weak (and non-significant) link was found with somatic complaints in childhood for non-personality disordered females, but no real associations were found that could support any major degree of masked depression in childhood. It could be that the wrong symptoms were recorded or used in the study. However adult depression has been shown to relate to the childhood symptom, and the childhood symptom when plotted against age of first presentation shows a deep U-shaped curve. If a similar graph is plotted,

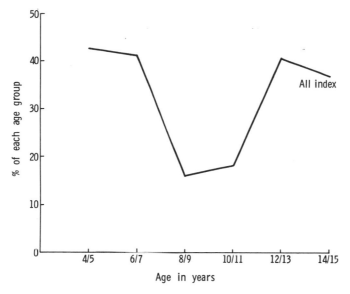

Graph 6.5 (a). Relationship between age at first presentation in childhood and diagnosis of depression in adult life.

but for all adults with depression against age at first childhood presentation, it is seen that once again the typical U-shape is found (Graphs 6.5a and b, 6.6a, b, and c). These graphs do not depend on the nature of the childhood symptom and it would be expected that 'masked depressions' would make the curve much flatter.

OTHER CHILDHOOD ANTECEDENTS OF ADULT DEPRESSION

The most striking feature was the relative lack of clear patterns between childhood symptomatology and adult depression. Table 6.8 (p. 66) summarizes some of the findings. Surprisingly little help is gained from the links with childhood symptoms. Sleep disturbance fits with a picture of adult depression, but this symptom occurred in a high proportion of all index cases. Sulkiness and stubbornness might have interesting implications as depressive antecedents, but for both the descriptive data tended to be less than precise and such character traits may best be investigated in a prospective study using more sophisticated rating scales.

Parental status Of the associations found the status of the parents is perhaps the most interesting. No link was found with loss of a parent by death or separation. The data were capable of showing one, as such a link

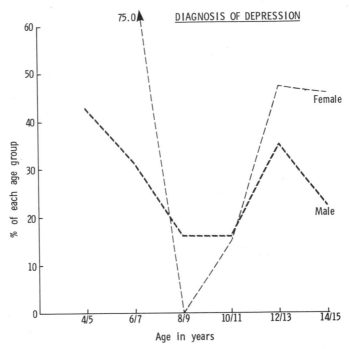

Graph 6.5 (b). Relationship between age at first presentation in childhood and diagnosis of depression in adult life according to sex.

was found for adult personality disorder. A connection was found, though, with the mental health of parents during childhood.

Data concerning parental mental health was on the whole poorly recorded at least with regard to detail. In this study therefore wide inclusion criteria were used, descriptions suggestive of anxiety states or depression being scored as unwell, whether or not the parent had received formal treatment. None the less a clear association was found, particularly for the adult symptom of depression, and further analysis showed that the association varied according to age, sex, and sex of parents.

PSYCHIATRIC HEALTH OF MOTHER

Depression in adult life was found to be associated with childhood contact with a mother with psychiatric disturbance. This applied to index cases of either sex, but only those who presented in childhood aged 12 or less (Table 6.9). The association is strongest with the adult symptom of depression, and 50 per cent of both male and female adults complaining of depression had a mother unwell if they presented before the age of 13,

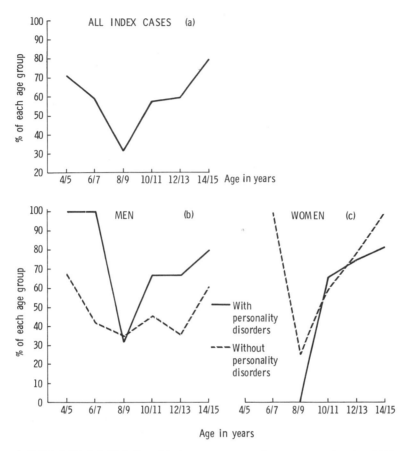

Graph 6.6 (a) (b) (c). Relationship between age at first presentation in childhood and complaint of depression in adult life.

as compared with 31 per cent of non-depressed males and 8.3 per cent of non-depressed females. As about 30 per cent of all child controls below age 13 also had a psychiatrically unwell mother, it seemed that disturbance in the mother only slightly increased the risk of adult disturbance, but had a determining effect on the nature of adult illness within the index group. The link was to a small extent also present for older boys, but entirely absent for older girls.

PSYCHIATRIC HEALTH OF FATHER

The effect of psychiatric illness in fathers differed from that in mothers; whereas the latter was connected with the age of the child, the former related more to the sex. For the symptom of depression in adult life a link

Table 6.8. *Index/Control differences for childhood items according to an outcome for a diagnosis of depression*

	Index			
	Adult depression		Child	Depressed
	Absent	Present	Controls	Control
All cases (male and female)	(N=111)	(N=50)	(N=161)	
	%	%	%	
Alternative parental care	9.0	4.0	11.2	
Sulkiness	27.9	56.0	35.4	$p<0.01$
Restless and over-active	27.9	12.0	21.7	$p<0.05$
Sleep disturbance	32.4	40.0	22.4	$p<0.01$
Depression (childhood symptom)	24.3	38.0	22.4	$p<0.05$
Younger children	(N=72)	(N=29)	(N=101)	
	%	%	%	
Psychiatric illness in either parent	40.3	69.0	41.2	$p<0.05$
Psychiatric illness in mother	30.6	58.6	30.7	$p<0.05$
Male children	(N=72)	(N=26)	(N=98)	
	%	%	%	
Psychiatric illness in father	12.5	26.9	17.4	N.S.
Female children	(N=39)	(N=24)	(N=63)	
	%	%	%	
Stubbornness	18.0	54.2	20.0	$p<0.01$

was found between paternal psychiatric disturbance and male index cases, irrespective of age at childhood presentation (Table 6.10): 26 per cent of adult males complaining of depression had a disturbed father, as compared with only 6.3 per cent of non-depressed males. The pattern for the diagnosis of depression is similar but fails to reach levels of statistical significance.

DIFFERENCES BETWEEN DEPRESSIVE NEUROSIS AND OTHER NEUROTIC DISORDERS

At various times in the text reference has been made to the difference between depressive disorders and other adult neurotic disorders in the relationship to continuities from childhood. Table 6.11 shows this in

Table 6.9. *Psychiatric health of mother and adult depression: Index cases presenting in childhood before age 13*

In childhood	Adult symptom			
	Male		Female	
	No depression	Depression	No depression	Depression
(a) Symptom of depression				
Mother well	24	18	11	9
Mother ill	11	18	1	9
Total	35	36	12	18
Male and female together χ^2 6.35, d.f.1, $p<0.05$				
(b) Diagnosis of depression				
Mother well	33	9	17	3
Mother ill	18	11	4	6
Total	51	20	21	9
Male and female together χ^2 6.87, d.f.1, $p<0.01$				

Table 6.10. *Psychiatric health of fathers and adult depression. All male index cases*

	Adult symptom	
	Absent	Present
In childhood:		
Father well	45	37
Father ill	3 *(6.3%)*	13 *(26.0%)*
Total	48	50

χ^2 6.99, d.f.1, $p<0.01$.
Percentages shown are of column totals.

terms of the relationship to broad groups for childhood diagnosis. First, far fewer of those with non-depressive neurosis had not also been diagnosed as showing emotional disorder in childhood, 6.5 per cent, as compared with 32 per cent. Secondly, when delinquency and conduct disorder are considered together, those with depression in adult life were far more likely to have shown these in childhood than all other forms of adult neurotic disorder, 64 per cent, as compared with 22.6 per cent, a difference significant at the 0.1 per cent level. Thirdly, delinquency, the severest form of conduct disorder, was the childhood diagnosis in 18 per cent of depressed adults, but none of the adults with non-depressive neuroses.

Table 6.11. *Childhood diagnosis of adults with neurotic disorders*

	Adult diagnosis			
	Non-depressive neurosis		Neurotic depression	
Childhood diagnosis	Male	Female	Male	Female
Neurotic disorder	9	16	9	11
Mixed conduct/neurotic	4	0	8	6
Conduct disorder	2	1	5	4
Delinquency	0	0	6	3
Total cases	14*	17	26**	24
Cases with no childhood neurosis	1	1	9	7

(a) *One case with conduct disorder and obsessional neurosis in childhood.
**Two cases with delinquency and neurotic disorder.

(b) The last row shows separately the number of cases with no diagnosis of neurotic disorder in childhood.

For depressive v non-depressive adult disorder χ^2 7.55 d.f.1, $p < 0.01$.

(c) Presence of diagnosis of neurotic disorder in childhood, for all cases χ^2 5.82, d.f.1, $p < 0.05$.

(d) Presence of any disturbed conduct disorder in childhood for all cases χ^2 13.15, d.f.1, $p < 0.001$.

SUMMARY

The study showed a variety of positive and negative results relating to depressive disorders in cases with psychiatric disorder in childhood and adult life.

1. Reported incidence of depression varies in different studies, but the rates here are comparable with those of other studies.

2. The rates for incidence are consistent with the opinion that most depressed adults do not have overt childhood antecedents and probably that most depressed children do not go on to have psychiatric disturbance in adult life.

3. Where illness occurs both in childhood and adult life there is strong continuity for the symptom of depression once it has occurred in childhood.

4. Continuity of the childhood symptom to the adult diagnosis of depression is found only as a weak association.

5. A depressive syndrome generated from a fixed symptom list in childhood showed strong continuity to a similar syndrome in adult life.

6. The presence of depressed mood in childhood was essential for the continuity of the childhood syndrome to adult depression.

7. Only a few childhood symptoms commonly preceded adult depression.
8. Loss of a parent did not correlate with adult depression.
9. Psychiatric disorder in parents did correlate with adult depression.
10. Depressive neurosis 'behaves' differently from other neurotic disorders with respect to child adult continuities.
11. The U-shaped pattern for age-related incidence of depression in childhood is remarkably constant no matter what marker for depression was used.

DISCUSSION AND CONCLUSION

Some clear continuities were found between childhood and adult depression, the two strongest links being for the symptom of depression and for a generated syndrome, designated syndrome X in childhood and syndrome Z in adult life. The clinical diagnosis of depression in adults in contrast showed only weak continuity from childhood. The findings here raise important questions about the identification of depression in childhood and adult life and the connection between the two. The continuity seems fairly clear in this study and it is surprising that others have failed to find it (Graham, 1974; Poznanski, 1980). In part this may be due to the failure to separate depression from other emotional disorders in longitudinal studies; neither Pritchard and Graham (1966) nor Robins (1966) did so. Part of the explanation may also be that childhood depression does not appear generally to increase the risk for adult morbidity and, more commonly, depression arises in adults without preceding childhood disturbance; the comparison with controls in this study demonstrates this. The association is only found when disturbance occurs both in childhood and adult life, for whatever reason.

The identification of valid depressive syndromes in childhood remains problematic. Pearce (1974) derived his syndrome using factor analysis, and syndrome X is based on his findings, but it can be seen that with regard to longitudinal continuity syndrome X behaves very much like the childhood symptom of depression. Similarly, the derived syndrome Z in adults also tended to 'behave' like the adult symptom of depression. This was in fact checked by comparing cross tabulations with other childhood variables. It is also possible that the continuity between the two is merely the sum of the continuities for the individual symptoms. None the less syndrome X would appear to have some validity as judged by Pearce's work and both syndromes X and Z require the presence of at least three items. As such, syndrome Z offers distinct advantages over the clinical diagnosis in adult life. Two reasons for this seem likely, first, it was systematically consistent, being generated from rigid criteria; secondly, it was independent of any other diagnosis whether that was a coexisting non-depressive neurosis or a personality disorder. Paykel and Prussoff (1977) used factor analysis to try to define subgroups in adult depression and separated four groups. They showed differences between those with onset in young adult life, middle age, and old age. There is some similarity between the subjects in this study and the two young groups in Paykel and Prussoff's study, and certainly in both there was often an admixture of personality problems. It is possible therefore that the continuity from childhood involves a particular form of depression occurring in young adults and with features similar to childhood drepression.

Another issue concerns the ways in which depressive disorders may be manifest in childhood as a wide variety of symptoms have been attributed to depression. In this study anxiety, aggression, and depression each had their own continuities and though these frequently overlapped there was nothing to suggest that depression had a direct continuity from either of the other two. That anxiety as a symptom appears in association with depression is well described (Tyrer, 1979) but, at least for adults, Schapira and colleagues (1972) found significant differences between the symptomatology and prognosis for groups given a clinical diagnosis of anxiety state or depression. Drotar (1974) and Lesse (1974) both attributed some delinquency and aggression to depression in childhood, but whilst the two are related in a way that delinquency does not relate to other emotional disorders this is a coexistence rather than evidence for continuity between the two.

In this study somatic syndromes did show some link with adult depression, but the association is weak and does not support somatic symptoms as being important masking symptoms for depression (Frommer & Cottom, 1970). Syndrome Y was similar in its criteria to depressive syndrome X but did not require the mandatory presence of depressed mood. For those without depressed mood, syndrome Y did not differ in associations from those without any form of childhood depression. There was therefore no evidence from this either to support the concept of masked depression in childhood in the absence of depressed mood. Kolvin and Nicol (1979) in their review considered that depressive equivalents should only be included (as depression) if the dysphoric symptoms are sufficiently prominent.

Childhood family life and adult depression. The relationship between loss of a parent and adult depression has been the subject of very many studies (Bowlby, 1961; Brown, 1961; Pitts *et al.*, 1965; Gregory, 1965) some arguing for a link and some against it. In this study no link was found between loss of a parent by any means, and adult depression.

Brown and Harris (1978) found evidence that loss of a mother before the age of eleven acts as a vulnerability factor rather than being directly aetiological. Brown's sample was very different from that used here, and the study has in fact been the subject of critical comment on method and conclusions (Tennant & Bebbington, 1978). More recently, Crook and Elliott (1980) reviewed the literature and also came to the conclusion that there was little evidence to substantiate a link. Graham (1981) did comment that Freud drew a parallel between the psychological process of mourning and of depression and that there is at times an assumed link in the psychopathology of these. In a retrospective study of depressed adults (Crook *et al.*, 1981), however, a link between parent–child relationships and adult depression was found, and this is more consistent with the findings here of a link with parental mental health.

Not quite half of all cases were noted to have some psychiatric disturbance in one or both parents, but no differences were found between the whole index and child control groups so that though parental mental illness might be associated with childhood disturbance, it did not in this study relate to any overall increased risk for adult life. This is in keeping with the findings of other studies (Robins, 1966; Sundby & Kreyberg, 1968; Rutter, 1966). Rutter compared the incidence of psychiatric disturbance in parents of children referred to a psychiatric department, with those referred to a dental clinic and found figures of 20 per cent for the former and 6 per cent for the latter, but neither Robins nor Sundby and Kreyberg found evidence for any link between parental mental illness and the overall prognosis. The results here suggest a more complex picture with regard to outcome. First, when all possible outcomes were considered, psychiatric disorder in parents was mainly associated with the later development of depression; secondly, this applied more to children aged 13 or less; thirdly, most but not all of the effect was due to illness in the mother, and finally there was some evidence that illness in fathers was more associated with later depression in male children of all ages.

Rutter (1966) also found evidence for a differential effect according to sex of parent and child with regard to childhood disturbance. Older children are beginning to separate themselves from their parents and may be less affected by an abnormal parent. It is understandable that mothers should have a greater impact on younger children of both sexes, as they are more involved in early child care. Fathers, too, may provide abnormal models for male children.

A harder question to answer is why depression should be the psychiatric disturbance associated with parental illness. Corroborative evidence is hard to find; Greenhill and Shopsin (1979) did find a higher incidence of affective disturbance in offspring of disturbed parents, but, unfortunately, though the mean age of the offspring was 22.4 years, the group was selected for affective illness in the parents. Though in this study the nature of the parental illness was not recorded in detail, though many parents might have been depressed, many other disorders, including anxiety states and psychoses, were certainly represented. Rutter (1979) felt that the evidence was against any particular pattern of disturbance in the children and also that the effect was largely via the accompanying family disturbance. If this were so, the outcome for parental physical and psychiatric disturbance would be more similar. Rutter did also comment on the importance of the involvement of the child in the parents' illness and here there is a marked difference in the effect; absent parents being connected with more uncontrolled behaviour, contact with a disturbed parent being connected with a vulnerability to later depression.

7. Continuities for obsessional disorders in childhood and adult life

Ritualistic behaviour is common in childhood and usually does not cause disability or persist. However, care was taken as far as possible to exclude such behaviour from the rating of the symptom of obsessions or compulsions, and to include only pathological behaviour. This was defined here as repetitive intrusive thoughts or repetitive actions recognized by the subject.

Obsessional disorders are rare both in childhood (Hollingworth *et al.*, 1980) and adult life (Marks, 1973) so that the high incidence of the symptom in the index group was particularly striking. The index/control differences were some of the clearest found in the study and separate consideration is therefore given here to this type of disorder.

PREVALENCE

Obsessions occurred as a symptom in more than twice as many index children (15.4 per cent) as control children (6.2 per cent). Though numbers were small, analysis according to age, sex, and later development of personality disorder showed that this was the same for all subgroups. In contrast, the diagnosis of obsessional neurosis was made in similar proportions of index cases and child controls, 6.2 per cent and 4.4 per cent.

In adult life obsessions also occurred as a symptom in many more index cases (19.3 per cent) than adult controls (8.1 per cent). Again, the diagnosis was made less often and in similar proportions in index cases and controls (Table 7.1).

CHILD–ADULT CONTINUITY

Symptom of obsessions

The association between the symptom of obsession in childhood and in adult life was one of the strongest found in the whole study (Table 7.2). Over 70 per cent of index cases with the symptom in childhood showed it again in adult life, whereas under 10 per cent of children without the symptom first showed it as an adult. Viewed from adult life, 60 per cent

Table 7.1. *Prevalence of obsessions as a symptom and diagnosis in index cases and controls*

	Child controls (N=161) (%)	Index cases (N=161) (%)	Adult controls (N=161) (%)
Obsessions in childhood			
Symptom	6.2	15.4	
Diagnosis	4.4	6.4	
Obsessions in adult life			
Symptom		19.3	8.2
Diagnosis		6.2	2.5

Obsessional symptom index vs child control χ^2 7.21 d.f.1, $p<0.01$.
Obsessional symptom index vs adult control χ^2 8.53 d.f.1, $p<0.005$.

Table 7.2. *Obsessions as a symptom in childhood and adult life*

	Adult life obsessions		
	Absent	Present	Total
Childhood obsessions			
Absent	123	13 (9.6%)	136
Present	7	18 (72.0%)	25
Total	130	31	161

χ^2 52.96 d.f.1, $p<0.0005$.
Percentages shown are of each childhood group.

of those with the symptom had a similar symptom as a child, but only 5 per cent of those without the adult symptom had childhood obsessions. Indeed, examination of the notes of this last group suggested that the nature of the phenomenon was less clear in some of these.

The data is presented for the whole group of 161 individuals but analysis was carried out according to various criteria, including age, sex, and presence of personality disorder in adult life. Though the strength of the association varied a little among these subgroups, the general pattern was the same for all.

When the figures for the symptom continuity are taken in conjunction with the comparison with controls it is clear that the symptom of obsessions in childhood is of prognostic significance. Of the 322 control cases (161 child and 161 adult) 7.1 per cent showed the symptom as compared with 23.6 per cent of the index cases who showed the symptom at some point, if the whole case record is considered. The controls were only a proportion of all patients attending so that an exact risk could not be calculated, as the child controls undoubtedly contained some individuals who later showed illness. None the less these results indicate a raised risk for the symptom in adult life once they have occurred in childhood.

DIAGNOSTIC CONTINUITY

Of six boys and four girls given a diagnosis of obsessive–compulsive neurosis during childhood, only four received the same diagnosis again in adult life. A further six adults were given the diagnosis in adult life but not in childhood. Table 7.3 summarizes the diagnostic links for the sixteen index subjects.

Ten children were given the diagnosis and of these five were later said to show other forms of neurotic disorder, mainly depression, even though four showed obsessional symptoms. In one case the adult diagnosis was alcoholism only, and it might be speculated that the alcohol relieved the symptom. Similarly, three of the six given the diagnosis only in adult life had shown obsessional symptoms in childhood, but had been diagnosed as having an 'unspecified' emotional disorder.

The childhood/adult continuity for the symptom of obsessions is clearly stronger than for the diagnosis. Examination of the case notes suggested that the main reason for this was simultaneous presence of other symptoms that competed for the diagnostic label. It was noted also that of the sixteen given the diagnosis at some time four were said to show conduct disorder in childhood and seven personality disorder in adult life. The childhood/adult continuity for antisocial behaviour seemed to be independent of the emotional/neurotic continuities present in the same individuals.

Table 7.4 shows diagnostic labels applied to those cases where the symptom was present but the diagnosis not given either in childhood or adult life. The first six cases show how the symptom continuity appeared irrespective of very varied diagnostic grouping.

DISCUSSION

The data concerning obsessional disorder show several important findings, including a high incidence in the index group, strong continuity from childhood to adult life and clearer differences for the symptom compared with the diagnosis.

The rates found here for a diagnosis of obsessional disorder of about 6 per cent of index cases both in childhood and adult life are not too dissimilar either to those for controls, or reported in the literature. The

Table 7.3. *Diagnostic correlations for obsessive/compulsive neurosis in childhood and adult life*

Childhood				Adult		
Case	Sex	Age	Diagnosis	Age	Diagnosis	
4824	M	7	+conduct disorder	25	Alcoholism	+PD
4823	M	8	+conduct disorder	26*	Anxiety neurosis	
4821	F	13*		23*	Unclassified neurosis	
5022	M	11*		25*		+PD
5823	F	15*	Obsessive/compulsive neurosis	25*	Depressive neurosis	
4722	F	13*		25		
5023	F	14*		21*		
6024	M	15*		21*		
5402	M	10*		20*		
5306	M	14	+developmental disorder	27*		+PD
5623	M	7		19*		+PD
5209	M	8*	Mixed conduct/emotional disorder	20*	Obsessive/compulsive neurosis	+PD
3621	F	11		41*		+PD
5210	F	15*		19*		+PD
5523	F	12	Unspecified neurosis	22*		
3202	F	15*		24*		

*Indicates presence of obsessions as symptom as child or adult.
+Indicates second diagnosis.
PD = Personality Disorder.

Table 7.4. *Cases with symptom of obsessions but not given the diagnosis*

Case	Sex	Age	Child diagnosis	Adult diagnosis	Obsessions present in	
					Child	Adult
5805	M	14	Schizophrenia	Schizophrenia	*	*
5502	M	12	Unspecified neurosis	Schizophrenia	*	*
4622	M	15	Mixed conduct/ neurosis	Antisocial personality disorder	*	*
5303	M	12	Unspecified neurosis/enuresis	Anxiety neurosis alcoholism	*	*
5103	M	5	Mixed conduct/ neurosis	Depression and antisocial	*	*
5703	F	15	Unspecified neurosis	Unclassified neurosis/immature personality disorder	*	*
5101	M	11	Unspecified neurosis	Phobic	*	
4701	M	8	Unspecified/ delinquency	Depressed/ personality disorder	*	
5208	M	5	Mixed conduct/ neurosis	Antisocial personality disorder	*	
5301	M	15	Unspecified	Depression	*	
4501	F	7	Mixed conduct/ neurosis and enuresis	Depression/ immature personality disorder	*	
5403	F	15	Manic depressive	Schizophrenia	*	
5824	M	8	Delinquency	Drug addiction/ personality disorder		*
5901	M	11	Mixed conduct/ neurosis/develop- ment disorder	Depression/ personality disorder		*
4723	M	10	Conduct disorder	Manic depression		*
4802	M	14	Enuresis	Depression/ immature personality disorder		*
5828	M	12	Delinquency	Depression/ immature personality disorder		*
5830	F	14	Unspecified neurosis	Depression		*
5701	F	11	Unspecified neurosis	Phobic/immature personality disorder		*
5404	F	15	Unspecified neurosis	Phobic/immature personality disorder		*
5002	F	10	Unspecified neurosis	Unclassified neurosis		*
5601	F	10	Delinquency	Immature personality disorder		*

rate in child controls was actually 4.4 per cent, and figures from other authors give rates of around 2 per cent (Judd, 1965; Adams, 1973). In absolute numbers this does not represent a great difference, and both authors required "a constellation of obsessive–compulsive symptoms" to be present, but no other significant disorder, criteria which might exclude some included here. Rutter (Rutter *et al.*, 1970) gave a higher rate of 5 per cent. The rate for adult controls, 2.5 per cent, is in keeping with the prevalence for patient populations given by Marks (1973).

Though it might be argued that the diagnostic rates of 6.0 per cent are three times higher than most other figures, this pales into insignificance when compared with the findings for the symptom alone. At some point in their lives (in the time span of the study) approximately 25 per cent of index cases showed the symptom of obsessions, and this is reflected in the comparison with both control groups.

Most other authors have found a bad prognosis for obsessional disorders (Lo, 1967; Warren, 1965; Hollingworth *et al.*, 1980), but it is suggested here that the presence of the symptom alone, irrespective of other coexisting symptoms is of greater prognostic significance than the diagnosis. Some caution, however, is required as the controls are drawn from a pool of some 4800 cases and if a rate of only 4 per cent is used, then some 200 other cases also showed obsessions.

The continuity from childhood to adult life for the symptom is impressive. Once occurring in childhood 72 per cent had the same symptom again when illness recurred, irrespective of the general nature of that illness. Pollitt (1957) observed that a high proportion of adults with obsessional disorder had a similar episode in childhood, and Kringlen (1965) in a retrospective study put the figure at 50 per cent. The figure of 58 per cent found here supports this.

The variations from study to study in all aspects of obsessional disorders would seem to stem, at least in part, from the way in which the disorder was defined. Surprisingly, follow-up studies have tended to look for persistence of the symptom even when more 'diagnostic' criteria had been used for the onset of the illness. Certainly many children show ritualistic behaviour that wanes with time, but care was taken here to include only those in whom a symptom was seen as alien and disabling.

The symptom could be merely a phenomenon occurring in various illnesses and, to some extent, this would seem to be true, as three cases developed clear psychotic illness, two of them being diagnosed at the time of first attendance. More striking, however, is the way in which obsessions occurred with a wide range of other symptoms, and the presence of depression, phobias, antisocial behaviour, etc., determined the diagnosis rather than there being any essential differences in the obsessional component. Hollingworth and colleagues (1980) used as one of their criteria for diagnosis 'No symptoms of other major psychiatric disorder', but the findings here would indicate that such cases may be pure in some way but are also atypical. It is suggested that the symptom of obsessions represents a disorder 'mechanism' in its own right, whatever the coexisting psychopathology.

The association with psychosis merits some further note. Three cases with the symptom of obsessions received the diagnosis of schizophrenia in adult life, two having been diagnosed as psychotic in childhood. This would appear to give a rate of 12 per cent for an outcome of psychosis, but again it has to be noted that there were potentially 255 cases among all children attending so that a figure of closer to 1 per cent is indicated. Other studies also show schizophrenia as a definite but uncommon outcome for obsessions (Pollitt, 1957; Hollingworth *et al.*, 1980).

8. Conduct disorder and personality disorder

Research over a number of years has shown that in children various anti-social behaviours tend to occur together in 'clusters' to form an apparent entity, at least distinct from emotional disorders (Jenkins & Glickman, 1946; Collins & Maxwell, 1962; Wolff, 1971). Such conduct disorder also has a relatively poor prognosis particularly for an outcome of personality disorder (Robins, 1966; West, 1969; West & Farrington, 1977). The data concerning this form of childhood behaviour and adult personality disorder are therefore drawn together in this chapter.

CONDUCT DISORDER AND DELINQUENCY IN CHILDHOOD

The term 'conduct disorder' usually refers to all forms of antisocial behaviour in children and 'delinquency' is in fact a legal, rather than psychiatric, term. Delinquency, however, is used here to denote conduct disorder occurring in a wider social setting. It was also found that many children showed behaviour that could not be classified as either anti-social or emotional but seemed to be a mixture of both. Such disturbance was classified as 'mixed conduct and emotional disorder'.

There was remarkably little difference in the incidence of any of these groups between index cases and child control cases (Table 8.1). Indeed, the only childhood item relating to antisocial disorder that differed between the whole index group and controls was aggression in boys, which occurred in 37.5 per cent of the former and 24.5 per cent of the latter, ($p < 0.05$). This lack of separation from the controls applied to the

Table 8.1. *Conduct disorder and delinquency in index cases and child controls*

	Boys ($N=98$)		Girls ($N=63$)	
	Index	Controls	Index	Controls
Mixed conduct/emotional	24	15	8	17
Conduct disorder/and delinquency	43	45	15	14

whole group, and it will subsequently be seen that important differences appear when the index group is divided according to outcome of personality disorder. However, the main implications are that the majority of antisocial children did not return to psychiatric services in adult life and those that did seemed only to differ in greater aggression.

PERSONALITY DISORDER IN ADULTS

The classification of personality disorder in adults is a subject of considerable disagreement (Scott, 1960; Sim, 1968; Walton & Presley, 1973; Liss *et al.*, 1973; Tyrer & Alexander 1979), and a system of distinct and valid categories is hard to find. In this study two main categories of antisocial/aggressive and immature/inadequate were used initially, based on a classification by Henderson (1939). If personality disorder was thought to be present a forced choice between these two had to be made. Two additional categories of alcoholism or drug abuse and sexual deviation could also be used as a separate diagnosis. In practice, the distinction between the two main groups was far from clear with most cases falling somewhere in the middle of what appeared to be a continuum.

Table 8.2 gives the figures for all of the categories of personality disorder used. The index group showed some form of personality disorder significantly more often than controls ($p < 0.01$), and the difference is made up predominantly by an excess of aggressive/antisocial personality disorder in men and inadequate/immature personality disorder in women. Though there may be discrete groups within personality disorder as a whole, much of the difference between the two main categories

Table 8.2. *Personality disorder in index cases and adult controls*

	Male		Female	
	Index $N=98$	Controls $N=98$	Index $N=63$	Controls $N=63$
No P.D.	25.5	33.7	36.6	62.0
Aggressive	43.0	23.5	4.8	6.4
Inadequate	27.6	31.6	57.1	27.0
Alcoholism	11.2	14.3	4.8	6.4
Sexual deviation	10.2	13.3	0	0

Figures shown are percentages of each column total.
For presence or absence of personality disorder:
Male χ^2 1.57, d.f.1, NS.
Female χ^2 8.13, d.f.1, $p < 0.01$.
NB: For alcoholism and sexual deviation the figures were aggregated from both diagnostic scales.

appeared to derive partly from sex differences and partly from differences in severity. Results are therefore given in terms of the presence or absence of personality disorder and reference to sub-categories is made only where it is particularly relevant.

The 23 men and 4 women in the control group who were said to show antisocial personality disorder were somewhat unexpected but the case records gave some indication that there was a qualitative difference from the majority of index cases receiving the same diagnostic label. Most appeared to be inadequate people who had none the less coped with the responsibility of adult life. A typical case history was of early marriage and children, failure to cope financially and socially, work failure, heavy drinking followed by petty crime and aggressive outbursts. The psychiatric presentation was often with anxiety and depression, and though some controls with personality disorder may have shown childhood disturbance not recollected or recorded the differences in severity and disablement seem to apply to most.

The data on individual symptoms further support these differences between index and control cases with personality disorder. Table 8.3 shows that controls were less often dependent, that is, more had left their parental home, were more often alcoholic, more likely to have physical sexual difficulties, that is, impotence or frigidity (in spite of a higher rate of marriage for men), and showed less antisocial behaviour but more depression.

The difference in competence was further reflected in the classification according to social class. Groups I, II, and III for social class include all skilled occupations. For those with personality disorder 37.0 per cent of

Table 8.3. *Comparison of index cases and control cases with personality disorder*

	Male		Female	
	Index $N=73$	Controls $N=65$	Index $N=40$	Controls $N=24$
Dependency on parents	35.6	15.4	47.5	25.0
Alcoholism	9.6	18.5	5.0	12.5
Physical sexual difficulties	8.2	16.9	22.0	25.0
Antisocial behaviour	60.2	36.9	12.5	20.8
Depression (symptom)	45.2	67.7	77.5	87.5
Depression (diagnosis)	26.0	35.4	42.5	75.0

Figures shown are percentages of each column total.
Rows are not mutually exclusive.

index men and 55.0 per cent of index females came into these three categories, as compared with 52.3 per cent and 66.7 per cent in controls.

Personality disorder was the only diagnostic group to occur more frequently in index cases as adults, whether with or without other psychiatric syndromes. It is not surprising that personality disorder in adults is associated with overt childhood disorder. Medinnus and Johnson (1969) commented that 'it might be expected that influences that occur earliest in life have the broadest impact on the individual's personality because they are incorporated into it and thus play a part in determining the effects of subsequent experience'. This fits well with the pattern seen for the age at which the index cases with personality disorder first presented (see Graph 5.1). Unlike all other adult diagnostic groups, the slope is downwards from the earliest age group of whom 90 per cent went on to personality disorder.

Two points emerge here with regard to classification of personality disorder. First, there is relatively little distinction on the level of a symptom presence or absence; that is, most adults with personality disorder seemed to have a variety of combinations of the same symptoms. The second factor is that though type of behaviour did not particularly separate index cases from controls with personality disorder, difference in severity of dysfunction was more noticeable. This was also one of the features that separated the two principal categories of personality disorder in the original classification used.

CONTINUITIES BETWEEN CHILD AND ADULT DISORDER

Outcome from childhood Conduct disorder could be placed in three categories, that is, delinquency, conduct disorder, and mixed conduct and emotional disorder. The first group contained 18 male and 4 female children, the second, 25 male and 11 female children, and the third, mixed group, 24 male and 8 female. Of the 90 children with any form of conduct disorder nearly all (82.2 per cent) went on to show personality disorder in adult life. The next most likely outcome, which could coexist with personality disorder, was depression which appeared in adult life in about 35 per cent. Psychosis was the principal adult illness in 11 per cent and non-depressive neurosis in only 7.8 per cent (Table 8.4).

Some differences between the subgroups of conduct disorder are worth noting. All delinquent children later showed personality disorder and none showed non-depressive neurosis. Depression related to all forms of childhood conduct disorder in a way in which other adult neurosis did not. Lastly, seven of the conduct-disordered children did not

Table 8.4. *Adult outcome for conduct disorder and delinquency*

Childhood diagnosis	P.D. only	All P.D.	Depression	Other neuroses	Psychoses
Male					
Delinquency *N*=18	61.1	100.0	33.3	0	5.6
Conduct disorder *N*=25	52.0	84.0	20.0	8	20.0
Mixed conduct/ emotional *N*=24	29.0	66.7	33.3	16.7	8.3
Female					
Delinquency *N*=4	25.0	100.0	75.0	0	0
Conduct disorder *N*=11	27.3	72.7	36.4	9.1	18.2
Mixed conduct/ emotional *N*=8	25.0	87.5	75.0	0	0

Figures shown are percentages of row total.
Columns are not mutually exclusive categories.

appear to have personality disorder by the time they reached adult life, and a brief look may be taken at these exceptions.

Four were diagnosed as psychotic (Cases 4621, 4623, 4723, 5926), each having shown varied but quite severe behavioural problems in childhood. For the three remaining cases (6029, 4801, 4823) case 6029 was a 13-year-old girl who was promiscuous as a child and for whom the decision not to deem personality-disordered as an adult seems marginal. The last two were both boys of above average intelligence. Case 4801 presented with encopresis and smearing at the age of 5. His other main disturbances of conduct were tempers and disobedience towards a rigid mother. He presented aged 20 with depression and somatic symptoms and his poor relationship with his 'rejecting' mother was again reported. However, he appears to have been functioning well socially otherwise. Case 4823 presented in childhood at the age of 8 with 'eye blinking' but also showed more widespread symptoms than the previous case. These included aggression, difficult behaviour in school, restlessness, disobedience, tempers, anxiety, tics, poor concentration, and obsessional thoughts. He returned at the age of 26 with a mixture of neurotic symptoms including anxiety, irritability, obsessions, phobias, panic attacks and somatic symptoms. Though he had impaired relationships with his family, he related well to others, showed no antisocial behaviour and worked as a skilled mechanic. Apart from the obsessions, his childhood history does not differ materially from other children who later showed personality disorder. There seems little to indicate why these two were different, except their intellectual ability and perhaps a rigidity of character.

ANTECEDENTS OF PERSONALITY DISORDER

Nearly all childhood diagnoses were made for those destined to show personality disorder, with the exception of psychosis (Table 8.5). Altogether, 69 men and 40 women were diagnosed as showing personality disorder of some form. Of these, 22 men and 10 women were thought not to show any other form of psychiatric disorder in adult life. In terms of the childhood antecedents there was remarkably little differ-

Table 8.5. *Selected childhood diagnoses and adult personality disorder*

	Adult			
	No P.D.	All P.D.	P.D. only	Psychosis
Male *Childhood*	(*N*=15)	(*N*=69)	(*N*=22)	(*N*=14)
All neurotic disorders	93.3 (*53.3*)	50.7 (*27.5*)	40.9 (*22.7*)	14.3 (*7.1*)
Conduct disorder and delinquency	53.3 (*13.3*)	73.9 (*50.7*)	77.3 (*59.1*)	57.1 (*35.7*)
Developmental delay	6.7	27.5	31.8	57.1
Female *Childhood*	(*N*=15)	(*N*=40)	(*N*=10)	(*N*=8)
All neurotic disorders	86.7 (*80.0*)	65.0 (*47.5*)	50.0 (*30.0*)	0
Conduct disorder and delinquency	13.3 (*6.7*)	47.5 (*30.0*)	50.0 (*30.0*)	25.0
Developmental delay	4.4	10.0	30.0	0

Figures shown are percentages of each column total.
Figures in brackets show percentages after exclusion of mixed conduct and neurotic disorder.
Columns 1, 2, and 4 add up to the group total.

ence between those with and those without other disorder. The evidence seems to indicate that other continuities into adult life are relatively independent and, for example, the presence of neurotic disorder related more to the continuity of neurotic symptoms than to the presence or absence of personality disorder.

A number of behavioural items in childhood occurred significantly more often in those destined to show personality disorder in adult life, compared with the rest of the index group (Table 8.6). The list, not surprisingly, was predominantly of various antisocial behaviours and is reflected in the different rates of childhood court appearance. Taken alone the P.D./No P.D. comparison would suggest that there was an increase of these behaviours in children going on to personality disorder, but comparison with the child controls indicates a different conclusion. For most items it was the non-personality-disordered index cases who had low rates in childhood, and the figures for those with personality disorder and the controls are similar. It seems that either the 'non-personality-disorder' cases are protected in some way or additional factors are necessary to produce personality disorder.

Aggression and educational retardation in males stand out as being different, in that they occurred more often in the future personality disorder group than in either of the two comparison groups. These items may therefore have a special causative role.

Table 8.6. *Antecedents of personality disorder*

Childhood data	No P.D.	P.D.	Child controls
All cases	(*N*=48)	(*N*=113)	(*N*=161)
Court appearance	4.2	21.2*	23.6
Stealing	8.3	38.9*	31.1
Truancy	8.3	29.2*	19.3
Lying	10.4	30.9*	23.6
Difficult at school	12.0	46.6 $p<0.05$	24.5
Histrionic behaviour	6.2	21.2*	14.3
Hysteria	0	5.3	4.4
Males	(*N*=25)	(*N*=73)	(*N*=98)
Aggression	12.0	46.6*	24.5
Educational retardation	47.4	76.7*	41.8
Younger males	(*N*=17)	(*N*=54)	(*N*=72)
Peer isolation	35.3	46.3	27.8
Overdependence	23.5	35.2	16.7
Destructiveness	5.9	27.8*	31.9

Figures shown are the percentage of each column total showing the childhood item.
For no P.D. vs. P.D. * denotes difference significant at 1 per cent level or better, except where stated.

The continuity for aggressive and violent behaviour has already been presented in Chapter 5. Briefly summarized, 40 per cent of children showing violence were again violent as adults; 88 per cent of violent children showed adult personality disorder and the remaining 12 per cent showed adult psychosis. For those showing aggressive behaviour in adult life only, there was some evidence for a link with developmental delay and neurological abnormality, but this did not account for all.

Some children showing aggression did not repeat this in adult life, but no particular pattern was seen. Those with aggression and no other anti-social behaviour were similar to those with a variety of antisocial behaviour in terms of outcome.

Educational retardation For male index cases 76.7 per cent of future personality disorder cases had shown educational retardation, as compared with 47.4 per cent of non-personality-disordered. The relationship between educational retardation and future personality disorder was sustained for both younger and older boys, but the pattern appears to be reversed for younger girls. The figures shown in Table 8.7 are only for those where some record of testing was found, and it is possible that the results are weighted in favour of those in whom developmental delay was suspected. Recalculation of the results, assuming that all of those not tested showed no evidence of delay, does not materially alter the overall pattern between index and control. For all cases, educational retardation then would occur in 22.9 per cent of non-personality-disorder, 49.7 per cent of personality disorder and 34.2 per cent of controls. This assumption does result in the non-personality-disorder/personality-disorder pattern becoming the same for girls below the age of 12 as for boys. For all girls the proportion is then 8.7 per cent of non-personality-disorder and 25.0 per cent of personality-disorder cases.

Court attendance Two further items of childhood behaviour, stealing and destructiveness, were not separately specified in the adult record, but both, like violence, only related to an outcome of personality disorder or psychosis. Another means of examining the links for antisocial behaviour is in terms of attendance at court (Table 8.8).

The majority of children who went to court went back to court as an adult in spite of the psychiatric attendance. Conversely, very few adults who did not go to court had been to court as a child. The figures for females are much smaller than for males, but the patterns are the same. The question does arise as to why some do not conform to this pattern and some of the exceptions are worth examining in further detail.

First, comparison can be made between those attending court for the first time in adult life and those 'repeaters' who went both as children and

Table 8.7. *Educational retardation and future personality disorder. Index/control comparison*

| | Index | | Control | Index | | Control |
	Non P.D.	P.D.		Non P.D.	P.D.	
	Male under 12			Male over 12		
Educational retardation						
Absent	8	12	28	2	2	18
Present	6 (42.9)	37 (75.5)	29 (50.9)	3 (60.0)	9 (81.8)	4 (18.2)
Total	14	49	57	5	11	22
	Female under 12			Female over 12		
Educational retardation						
Absent	2	13	15	8	11	16
Present	2 (50.0)	8 (38.1)	11 (42.3)	0	2 (18.2)	11 (40.7)
Total	4	21	26	8	13	27

Figures in brackets are percentages of column totals.
For Male Index P.D. vs. Control χ^2 16.93, d.f.1, $p < 0.0005$.
For Male Index non P.D. vs. P.D. χ^2 5.86, d.f.1, $p < 0.005$.

Table 8.8. *Court appearance in childhood and adult life*

	(All index cases)		
	Adult court appearance		
Child court appearance	Absent	Present	Total
Absent	101	34 (*25.2*)	135
Present	7	19 (*73.1*)	26
Total	108	53	161

χ^2 22.6, d.f.1, $p < 0.0005$.
Figures in brackets are percentages of row totals.

as adults (Table 8.9). The repeaters tended to show more varied and persistent antisocial behaviour both in childhood and adult life; as adults, almost half also showed drug or alcohol abuse. In contrast, the adult-only group more often were aggressive in childhood and for some this was the only recorded antisocial behaviour. Aggression also accounted for the higher rate of 'difficult in school'. As adults, first time court attenders showed more neurological and psychiatric disorder and over 25 per cent had sexual problems. Offences of those not showing persistent antisocial behaviour included such things as violent assault, arson, and stealing a car. If psychosis at any time, major sexual disorder (including homo-

Table 8.9. *Comparison of child and adult offenders with adult-only offenders*

	Adult only (*N*=34)	Child and adult (*N*=19)
Childhood		
Antisocial behaviour other than aggression	55.9	94.7**
Aggression	50.0	36.8
Aggression only	17.6	0.0
Difficult in school	47.0	36.8
Developmental delay	32.4	26.3
Adult		
Persistent antisocial behaviour	58.8	84.2*
Sexual problems	26.5	15.8
Alcohol/Drugs	26.5	47.4
Psychosis/Epilepsy	17.0	10.0

Figures are percentages of column totals.
χ^2 **$p < 0.01$. *$p < 0.05$.

sexuality), and epilepsy are added together, then these constitute 40 per cent of the first-time adult offenders and only 21 per cent of the juvenile and adult offenders.

Only two of the differences found reached statistical significance, but they do reflect the impression gained from the case notes that the first time adult offenders included more who were disabled in some manner and who were aggressive.

The case records of the seven subjects who attended court only in childhood were re-examined, as it was thought that these might be anti-social children who went on to adult psychosis. In fact, all such children reattended court in adult life in spite of the psychotic disorder. The seven children included four girls and three boys (cases 5822, 5607, 5305, 6029, 4924, 4701, 6028), of whom all but one were thought to show personality disorder, and the odd one out (case 6029) has already been noted as having only marginal evidence for a 'normal' personality in adult life. The four girls showed various forms of antisocial behaviour, including stealing, truanting, and promiscuity. The only identifiable constant feature in adult life was some form of sexual difficulty. The three boys all stole in childhood, but showed also a mixture of emotional and conduct disorder. As adults, immaturity, dependency, and emotional symptoms tended to predominate. One of them continued to steal and show strange behaviour, and the pattern of behaviour described suggested that he would eventually be charged, develop psychosis, or perhaps both.

So far, all data refer to the presence or absence of personality disorder, rather than the original two main categories of antisocial or immature. The reasons for this are given earlier, but some reference may be made here to these subgroups. The correlations with childhood items were not exactly the same for both categories, but generally in this respect anti-social and immature groups tended to be similar to each other and to the controls and different from the non-personality-disordered index cases (Table 8.10). Very few female index cases were said to show antisocial personality disorder, but in those with immature personality disorder antisocial behaviour was not uncommon.

It has been proposed that antisocial behaviour in adults is always preceded by antisocial behaviour in childhood (Robins, 1966, 1978). Here, however, eleven boys diagnosed as showing childhood emotional disorder were later specifically put in the category of antisocial person-ality disorder. Of these eleven, four were given a diagnosis in childhood of emotional disorder plus delinquency, one was diagnosed as obses-sional disorder plus conduct disorder, and three also showed childhood violence as a symptom. Three cases, however, were thought to show emotional disorder with no antisocial behaviour in childhood, but to

Table 8.10. *Correlation between childhood symptoms and type of personality disorder in males*

	Index			Control
	No P.D. (N=25)	Aggressive (N=42)	Immature (N=27)	(N=98)
Court appearance	4.0	31.0	18.5	27.6
Stealing	12.0	57.1	29.6	37.8
Lying	12.0	45.2	25.9	25.5
Truanting	16.0	50.0	11.1	23.5
Aggressive	12.0	54.8	29.6	24.5
Difficult in school	20.0	40.5	40.7	28.6
Tempers	44.0	50.0	51.9	39.8
Bullied	28.0	11.9	33.3	16.3
Dependence	4.0	23.8	18.5	24.5

Figures shown are percentages of total *N* for each column.

show antisocial personality disorder in adult life (Cases 5710, 5221 and 5401).

Case 5710 was an anxious effeminate boy who refused to go to school, in adult life he was isolated and miserable and stole, but was charged with indecent exposure. Case 5221 was an anxious dependent boy who refused to go to school. In adult life, after suspension from university, he stole to pay for abortions for girlfriends and was also said to be 'unreliable and untruthful'. These two were remarkably similar to one further case (case 5502) who went on to show adult schizophrenia. All three presented in childhood below the age of 13, were of above average intelligence, and refused to go to school. In adult life they all showed antisocial or aggressive behaviour and had some form of sexual disturbance. Case 5401 presented at the age of 9 as a small, dull boy who was dependent, fearful, and isolated. In adult life he was unable to hold a job and beat his wife. He differs from the others described here in that he received a childhood diagnosis of developmental delay as well as emotional disorder. One further case (case 3521) also showed no childhood antisocial behaviour and went on to adult personality disorder, of an inadequate/immature type. He presented at the age of 6 as being anxious, restless, and fidgety, was of average ability, and showed no school problems. In adult life he presented because of indecent exposure, was said to be inadequate, had many jobs, and married twice.

For these five cases there was no consistent pattern except early age of first presentation. The three with clearer antisocial behaviour in adult life all lived with their natural parents who were physically and psychiatrically well, though of older than average age (mean 33.7 years). They also showed dependence in childhood and an aversion to school.

ABNORMAL MATERNAL CARE

Most of the data relate to behaviour characteristics in childhood and their outcome in respect of adult personality disorder. A different type of link with childhood is concerned with the nature of maternal care, and several items referred to this.

The first of these concerned the physical well being of mothers. Almost all of the index cases who in adult life had no personality disorder·had had in childhood a mother who had been alive and physically well, but all who lost a mother by death did show personality disorder (Table 8.11). The striking feature is, though, that in these respects the personality disorder group are again similar to the controls. It is suggested therefore that the presence of a mother is protective rather than that absence is causative.

The second item concerned whether or not the natural mother was the primary caretaker. Similar numbers of index and control cases were adopted or fostered, but 15 of the 16 index cases who were not with their natural mother later showed personality disorder. The remaining one developed a psychosis in adult life. Two-thirds of the index cases in the care of their natural mother also showed personality disorder but the difference is significant at the 5 per cent level.

Finally, the presence or absence of a mother was also recorded in terms of any separation for more than four weeks either before or after the age of five years. For girls this criterion adds no further information, but for boys an association was again found for separation from both parents (Table 8.12). Once again it is the index patients without personality disorder who differ in their relatively low rate of early separation.

Table 8.11. *Maternal physical morbidity in childhood and adult personality disorder*

	Index		Control
	No P.D. (N=48)	P.D. (N=113)	(N=161)
Mother alive and well	91.7	67.7	77.6
Mother dead	0	6.2	6.2

Figures shown are percentages of each column total.
Index No P.D. vs. P.D. χ^2 10.58, d.f.1, $p < 0.001$.
Index No P.D. vs. Control χ^2 4.77, d.f.1, $p < 0.05$.

Table 8.12. *Separation from both parents for one month or more in male children*

	Index		Control
	No P.D. (*N*=25)	P.D. (*N*=73)	(*N*=98)
Separation before age 5	16.0	37.0	31.6
Separation after age 5	8.0	31.4	24.8
Separation at any time	24.0	67.1	56.1

No P.D. vs. P.D.
No P.D. vs. control χ^2 just fails to reach significance at 5% level.
Figures shown are percentages of total *N* for each column.

When those with physically ill mothers, those separated from their mother for more than one month, those who lost their mother by death, and those in alternative care for any other reason (later adoptions, fostering, and so on) are all added together there are 88 children after allowing for overlaps. Of these 88 children with deficient mothering, 73 later showed personality disorder, differing significantly from the rest of the index group (Table 8.13). This is a very strong association, with about half of those with mothers present and physically well showing personality disorder, but very nearly all those with this form of deficient mothering having personality disorder as the outcome.

DISCUSSION AND CONCLUSIONS

If one looks first at the outcome from childhood, most childhood anti-social behaviour occurred in similar proportions in index cases and controls. In the index cases though, the outcome was fairly predictably

Table 8.13. *Deficient mothering and personality disorder*

	Male		Female		All		Total
	No P.D.	P.D.	No P.D.	P.D.	No P.D.	P.D.	
Normal mothering	17	25	17	14	34	39	73
Deficient mothering	8	48	7	25	15	73	88
				Total	49	112	161

χ^2 male 8.66, d.f.1, $p < 0.05$.
χ^2 Female 7.26, d.f.1, $p < 0.01$.
χ^2 All 16.43, d.f.1, $p < 0.0005$.

personality disorder or psychosis. Aggression in childhood stood out as always predicting these two adult diagnoses in index cases, and as also occurring more often than in the controls. West and Farrington (1977) were also impressed by the role of aggression and commented that continuity of aggressive behaviour was probably higher than reported. Whether aggressiveness is innate, acquired by learning, or a morbid process cannot be determined here, but aggression in childhood would seem to deserve more consideration in its 'own right' rather than predominantly masking other aspects of behaviour.

Stealing and destructiveness were similarly associated with an adult outcome of personality disorder or psychosis and it was not surprising to find that court appearance in childhood was a strong predictor of court appearance in adult life. West and Farrington (1977) reported that 50.8 per cent of adults with a conviction had previously been convicted as children, as compared with 35.9 per cent in this study, but found that a somewhat lower proportion of children with convictions were reconvicted in adult life, 61 per cent, as compared with 73 per cent in this study. None the less the patterns are remarkably similar, considering the different designs of the studies. The continuity of antisocial behaviour has also been stressed by Robins (1966) who concluded that the most likely candidate for a later diagnosis of sociopathic personality would be 'a boy referred for theft or aggression, who has shown a diversity of antisocial behaviour ... at least one of which could be grounds for a Juvenile Court appearance'.

Comment has already been made on the exceptions to continuity particularly with regard to violence and court appearance. For those with disturbance in childhood but appearing antisocial for the first time in adult life some of the findings can be drawn together, though it must be remembered that for each the numbers were small and conclusions are therefore tenuous. None the less, two subgroups seem to appear, an impaired group who show violence and a group of dependent school refusers. Though hostility seems accepted as part of the school refusal syndrome Hersov (1977b) did not report an antisocial outcome in his review on prognosis.

Though certain patterns of childhood conduct were constantly linked to adult personality disorder, the reverse was not true. Adult personality disorder was preceded by a variety of childhood diagnoses. Explanations for this may be that a variety of adult disorders are being grouped together or that, in childhood, symptoms rather than personality traits were being used to make a diagnosis.

Various individual items did appear as more constant antecedents of adult personality disorder and, were it not for the use of controls, might have been designated as causative. However the control comparison showed that there was a relative lack of these items in the non-personality-disordered index cases. Other influences would therefore seem to be necessary to interact with these items to produce an adverse outcome.

A number of factors in this study related to family life and all of those that implied separation from or loss of a mother, were linked to an outcome of personality disorder. The association with 'abnormal mothering' was one of the strongest found in the whole study but the control comparison again shows that though the presence of a fit mother is protective the absence of a mother is not in itself sufficient to result in personality disorder. This proposes a rather different mechanism from the 'irreversible impact of deprivation' (Bowlby, 1951). Wolkind (1974b) studying institutionalized children found a high rate of antisocial behaviour and relationship difficulties. He suggested that the outcome was more connected with family factors than the institutionalization per se. Wolkind had also previously noted the differing effects of long term care on boys and girls (Wolkind, 1974a), and Cloninger and colleagues (1975) proposed a higher threshold for the effects of environmental factor for girls, as compared with boys. In this study small sex differences were found with regard to separation rather than to alternative care, but the indication also was that boys were more vulnerable.

Educational retardation showed a positive association with the development of personality disorder in both males and females, though it reached statistical significance only for males. Learning difficulties, particularly in the form of reading retardation have been shown to be linked to childhood conduct disorder (Rutter, 1970b). Rutter & Madge (1976) discussed various possible mechanisms underlying the association and put greatest weight on the effect on self-esteem and motivation. This would certainly fit the findings here that many of the children did not have the support and encouragement of an intact family. The link between educational performance and adult disorder has been shown for both psychosis (Offord & Cross, 1969; Schofield, 1959; Rutter & Garmezy, 1983) and also personality disorder (West & Farrington, 1977). West and Farrington's data actually referred to 'poor school achievement' in childhood and to cases 'convicted as both juvenile and adult'. They compared that group with non-delinquents and found rates of 24.2 per cent in the latter and 52 per cent in the former. Allowing for differences in inclusion criteria, this matches quite well with the 47 per cent and 76 per cent found here. Whether learning difficulties are due to intrinsic or environmental factors, it is difficult to ignore the work of Rutter and his colleagues (Rutter *et al.*, 1975; Berger *et al.*, 1975) who showed that school environmental factors are important in the genesis of disorder in children. Even if this is an interaction with intrinsic factors it points to a potential means of reducing adult morbidity.

At the onset of the study it proved difficult to find a satisfactory classification of subgroups in the overall 'category' of personality disorder. The results do not show one single consistent pattern and the variety of differences may shed some light on possible subgroups. This may be summarized as follows:

1. Most with personality disorder showed mixtures of dependence, immaturity, together with antisocial behaviour of some form.
2. Adults with personality disorder but no history of childhood disturbance were on the whole far more competent than those with childhood records.
3. Of those with childhood attendance there was tentative evidence for the presence of subgroups:
   (a) Those with a constellation of antisocial behaviours persisting over time.
   (b) Those with various dysfunctions, particularly neurological, presenting with predominantly aggressive behaviour, particularly as adults.
   (c) A group showing dependence in childhood with aversion to school and aggression in adult life, with sexual disorders.

9. Psychosis

In this study schizophrenia and affective psychosis were the two principal categories of psychotic disorder, both in childhood and in adult life. Though the numbers given these diagnoses were not large the size of the group was adequate to explore various issues. The clinicians at the childhood attendance could not know the outcome and it was therefore possible to examine differences between children recognized as showing psychosis and those not so recognized but eventually showing the disorder in adult life. The perspective of time further permitted an appraisal of the distinction made in young people between the two main types of psychotic disorder. Comparison is also made with the adult control group for evidence of differences between those with and without childhood antecedents.

Fourteen index adults were given a diagnosis of schizophrenia, 7 were given a diagnosis of affective psychosis and one was said to show an 'unspecified psychosis'. One further adult in the index group was given a research diagnosis of personality disorder, though the notes 'debated' between that and schizophrenia. These twenty-three cases comprise 14.3 per cent of the whole index group. Not all of these received a diagnosis of psychosis in childhood but all children with an identified psychosis continued into this adult group; Table 9.1 shows the overall summary. It is convenient to look first at the index group in childhood, then in adult life, and finally to return to the continuities between the two.

PSYCHOSIS IN CHILDHOOD

Including all forms of psychotic disorder, this category was used for ten index children (6.2 per cent) and four control children (2.5 per cent). Table 9.2 shows the index-control comparison divided by age. Of the ten children with psychosis over the age of 12, nine were in the index group, a difference significant at the 1 per cent level. This suggests that, for older children at least, the likelihood of recurrence of illness was quite high. The one child with psychosis over the age of twelve in the control group differed little from those in the index group and the possibility of return to other adult psychiatric services cannot be excluded.

Four of the nine index cases over 12 were said to have recovered and five improved at discharge so that in childhood a deteriorating course

Table 9.1. *Psychosis in childhood and adult life*

Childhood					Adult	
Case No.	Sex	Age	Diagnosis		Age	Diagnosis
5806	F	14	Schizophrenia		16	Schizophrenia
4601	F*	15	Schizophrenia		24	Schizophrenia
5805	M	14	Schizophrenia		28	Schizophrenia
5923	M*	8		**	18	Schizophrenia
5503	M	13	Organic B.D.	**	18	Schizophrenia
4921	M	8		**	25	Schizophrenia
4804	M	10		**	22	Schizophrenia
4623	M	14		**	21	Schizophrenia
4621	F	15	Conduct disorder		35	Schizophrenia
3701	M*	11			39	Schizophrenia
5808	M	13	Emotional disorder		19	Schizophrenia
5003	M	7		**	19	Schizophrenia
5502	M	12			21	Schizophrenia
5403	F	15	Manic depressive		19	Schizophrenia
6121	F*	13	Manic depressive		18	Manic depressive
3921	F*	14			23	Manic depressive
5804	F*	15	Schizophrenia		18	Manic depressive
5807	M*	14			17	Manic depressive
5922	M	12		**	20	Manic depressive
5926	F	13			21	Manic depressive
4723	M	10	Conduct disorder		25	Manic depressive
4703	M	4		**	17	Unspecified psychosis
5803	M*	15	Schizophrenia		21	Personality disorder

*Shows those with acute onset.
**Shows presence of developmental disorder.

had not yet commenced, whereas in adult life only one was said to have recovered, the others being unchanged or worse.

Of the four children with an identified psychosis below the age of twelve three were in the control group. One of the control children had an acute illness after an upper respiratory tract infection and medication reported in the notes as 'sulphur' drugs (presumably sulphonamides). However, that child had two further episodes that may have been more hysterical than psychotic in character, the notes indicating delusions and hallucinations in the first episode only. The remaining two control children both showed bizarre behaviour and developmental delay, in this resembling those index children destined to show adult psychosis but not so diagnosed in childhood.

Table 9.2. *Psychosis in childhood*

	Age under 12		Age over 12	
	Index	Control	Index	Control
Childhood psychosis present	1	3	9	1
Childhood psychosis absent	101	99	50	58

Under 12 χ^2 1.02, NS.
Over 12 χ^2 6.99, d.f.1, $p < 0.01$.

For older children the index-control difference is in keeping with most other studies with a bad prognosis for early onset psychosis (Masterson, 1958, 1967; Eggers, 1978). For younger children the results do not really give a clear finding. Though eight younger children went on to show psychotic disorder in adult life, only one was so diagnosed as a child, whereas three controls aged 12 or less appeared to show a psychosis. One of these three almost certainly had a short-lived psychosis related to treatment for an infection, and this may have been easier to identify as being acute and florid, but this explanation would not account for the other two.

Eggers (1978) was a little less pessimistic than most about outcome as he did find 20 per cent recovery at follow-up after 20 years. This, though, applied to those with onset over the age of 10. It can only be said that the two control cases either recovered or presented later elsewhere.

PSYCHOSIS IN ADULT LIFE

Psychotic disorders appeared in very similar proportions in index cases as adults and the adult controls. For males the figures were 14.5 per cent and 17.4 per cent respectively and for females 12.7 per cent and 11.1 per cent. When divided by type of psychosis the figures still remain similar, with 8.7 per cent of index cases and 7.5 per cent of controls showing schizophrenia and 4.3 per cent and 6.2 per cent showing affective psychosis.

The diagnostic symptoms could not really differ between index and controls as the same criteria were used for diagnosis in both, but the impression gained from the case notes was that the index cases were far more incapacitated and that the control cases were able to function more efficiently, at least up to the onset of the illness. The general similarity of figures for index and controls is to be expected; whereas early onset schizophrenia persists, there is a greater incidence after puberty.

OUTCOME FOR IDENTIFIED CHILDHOOD PSYCHOSIS

As noted above, ten children were said to show psychosis and, of these, nine went on to some form of psychotic disorder in adult life, so that for psychotic disorders as a whole an identifiably psychotic pattern of disturbance recurs as such. The one boy who was not given a diagnosis of psychosis in adult life presented with confusion and hallucinations at the age of 15, but when seen again at 21 showed no 'first rank' symptoms of schizophrenia. Considerable contemporary discussion none the less seems to have occurred concerning the nature of his disorder (Case 5803). It is of interest that the case note diagnosis in childhood was affective psychosis, whereas the research assessment was schizophrenia, this latter being made by both assessors before discussion.

When the nine identified in adult life as psychotic were divided according to affective psychosis or schizophrenia, agreement with adult diagnosis was not impressive. Three boys and four girls were given the diagnosis of schizophrenia in childhood, one boy (Case 5807) and two girls (Cases 3921 and 5804) later being diagnosed as manic-depressive in adult life. Of the two girls with a diagnosis of manic-depressive psychosis one was later given the same diagnosis but the other was subsequently said to show schizophrenia (Case 5403).

Thus, though the continuity for psychotic disorder was clear, the nature of the disorder between the choice of schizophrenia or affective psychosis was often changed between childhood and adult life.

From Table 9.1 it can be seen that there was some distinction according to the mode of onset. Seven of the ten cases diagnosed as psychotic in childhood had an acute onset. This included four of the seven adults with an affective psychosis (57 per cent) but only three of the fourteen adults with schizophrenia (21.4 per cent). Apart from the nature of onset there were few other distinguishing features to separate those with future schizophrenia from affective psychosis. If the four identified as suffering from schizophrenia in childhood who later went on to adult schizophrenia in adult life are compared with those going on to affective psychosis it was found that four of the former, but none of the latter had an illness lasting more than six months. So that an acute illness of short duration was more likely (3:1) to go on to affective psychosis. This however did not carry over into those cases not preceded by an identified childhood psychosis where there was no distinction between future affective psychosis and future schizophrenia. Depressed mood also shows some difference occurring in childhood in all three of the schizophrenia to affective psychosis group, but only one of the schizophrenia to schizophrenia cases. For all adults with psychosis depressed mood in childhood was recorded in five of the seven adults with affective psychosis, as compared with only four of the fourteen with schizo-phrenia. It can be seen that because of the greater numbers going on to schizophrenia, though affective psychosis tended to be preceded by a childhood psychosis of acute onset, short duration, and depressed mood, these symptoms could not be used to predict that outcome.

The two girls showing affective psychosis in childhood, (Cases 5403 and 6121) both were bright, had depressed mood and a duration of illness of more than six months. Case 5403 had explosive outbursts, saying 'sex, sex, sex, I can't think of anything else', and bouts of crying, expressing feelings of guilt. The research diagnosis agreed with the case-note diagnosis of 'endogenous depression'. At the age of 19, after four years of apparently normal mental health she became increasingly with-drawn over four months, presenting with inappropriate giggling, manner-isms, delusions, and lack of affect. She showed slow improvement over seven months and both research and case note diagnoses agreed on schizophrenia. Case 6121 was more clearly depressed and was diagnosed constantly as having a depressive illness. She did also show delusions, albeit of a morbid nature. The interval between the childhood attendance at age 13 and adult attendance aged 18 seems to have been marked by several minor episodes, mainly with a predominant affective component though she was said to have had paranoid delusions for a period of two weeks. At age 20 she was put on Lithium and remained well for 2 years. Unlike case 5403, who had a deteriorating course as an adult, she was well and effective between bouts of illness.

ANTECEDENTS OF ADULT PSYCHOSIS

As only 9 of the 22 index cases with psychosis in adult life were identi-fied as showing psychosis in childhood, the majority, 59.1 per cent, were given other diagnostic labels in childhood. A sex difference is apparent, though numbers are small. Of thirteen male adults with psychosis only 3 (23.1 per cent) were identified in childhood as psychotic, but six of the eight (75 per cent) of the females were. It was also found that all eight children who presented before age 13 (irrespective of symptomatology) were male.

SCHIZOPHRENIA

Of the fourteen adults given this diagnosis (ten male and four female) four were recognized as such in childhood and one was said to show 'manic-depressive psychosis'. The others received various diagnoses, but predominantly a mixture of developmental, conduct, and emotional disorders.

At a symptom level all four recognized as showing schizophrenia showed either delusions or hallucinations and these seem to have been the essential diagnostic criteria, as these cases were otherwise very similar to those not identified as psychotic. Table 9.3 shows that peer isolation, poor concentration, specific developmental delay, restlessness and violence were all more common in patients with future psychosis when compared with either the controls or those destined to show adult neurotic disorder. However, on these criteria there was a remarkable similarity to those destined to show personality disorder.

One symptom stood out for all those with future psychosis, that of incongruous behaviour. There was nothing to distinguish affective psychosis from schizophrenia on this criterion, which occurred in 59.1 per cent of the whole psychosis group. The incidence in the emotional disorder and personality disorder groups was 9.1 per cent and 7.8 per cent respectively and that in the child control group 12.4 per cent. This slightly higher figure for the control group is quite consistent with the previously noted 'impure' nature of the control, and indeed if a base rate of 9 per cent for this symptom is taken with the presence of four identi-

Table 9.3. *Index/Control differences for childhood data according to an outcome of psychosis in adult life*

	Index cases			Child control
	Adult diagnosis			
	Psychosis	Emotional disorder	Personality disorder	
	($N=22$)	($N=88$)	($N=51$)	($N=161$)
Peer isolation	54.6	29.6	47.1	28.0*
Poor concentration	45.5	28.4	37.3	26.1
Specific developmental delay	36.4	12.6	33.3	26.1
Restless & overactive	36.4	13.6	33.3	21.1
Violence	31.8	17.1	39.2	19.3
Hallucinations	18.2	0	2.0	1.9**
Incongruous behaviour	59.1	9.1	7.8	12.4***
Delusions	($N=13$)	($N=11$)	($N=36$)	($N=59$)
(older children)	38.5	6.1	8.3	1.7***

N for P.D. = Personality disorder only.
N for emotional disorder includes only those without P.D.
Figures shown are percentages of total, N, for each column.
For each childhood item comparing 'psychosis' with child control χ^2 *=$p<0.05$; **=$p<0.005$; ***=$p<0.0005$.

fiably psychotic children, then a figure of 12 per cent can be anticipated. The difference between the future psychotic group and the control (or any other index subgroup) is highly significant statistically.

Examination of the case notes indicated that the recording psychiatrists found it difficult to identify just what evoked that description of 'incongruous behaviour'. The overall impression gained was that the children were unpredictable in a way that could not be accounted for in terms of normal child behaviour and the immediate circumstances. The term 'incongruous behaviour' was actually included because it appeared in the contemporary case notes. Cases 4703, 4804, 3701 and 4921 give some examples of what was referred to. Case 4703 was a four-year-old boy who had bouts of prolonged laughter and incomprehensible speech. His case records gave a diagnosis of conduct disorder and motor speech defect. Case 4804 was a ten-year-old boy who was said to be violent, overactive, and attention-seeking; he was found one day dancing in the street. Case 3701 was an eleven-year-old boy presenting with school refusal and vomiting. He also had bouts of screaming and punching his chair; the case note diagnosis was of anxiety neurosis. The written case records suggested that the term 'incongruous' referred not just to such behaviour but also to a general difficulty in communication, and case 4921 illustrates this a little. He was aged eight and presented with truanting; the notes recorded that he was seen as odd by his peers and described him as 'like plate glass' with reference to rapport.

Overall, a general impression of future schizophrenics could be gained from the case notes. For the most part there was an insidious onset of a mixture of antisocial behaviour, social isolation, and poor concentration with failing school performance, together with an unpredictability that identified them as odd. Case 4804 showed this typically. In some the presence of delusions and hallucinations identified the illness as a psychosis, but otherwise most cases showed a similar pattern, whether or not the adult diagnosis was anticipated.

There was some indication of a differing pattern for those presenting first in early childhood (compared with later childhood). Examination of the case records of all younger children later identified as psychotic suggested that they were more likely to show bizarre behaviour and developmental delay irrespective of whether psychotic disorder was identified in childhood. Five of the six adults with schizophrenia who presented with any disorder at age 12 or less showed some form of developmental delay. The sixth actually had chronic physical disorder affecting his eyes. In contrast to this only one of the eight first presenting at age 13 or older showed developmental delay (Table 9.4).

Though developmental delay is more common in younger children the rates found were 40.3 per cent for controls and 32.4 per cent for all

Table 9.4. *Association between developmental delay and age of onset of symptoms in index cases developing psychoses (male and female cases)*

	Adult diagnosis			
	Schizophrenia		Manic depressive	
	Below 12	Above 12	Below 12	Above 12
No developmental delay	1	7	1	5
Developmental delay	5	1	1	0
Total	6	8	2	5
(Childhood psychosis	1	4	0	4)

For all adult psychosis younger v. older χ^2 7.29, d.f.1, $p < 0.01$.
Bracketed figures show the number of children who were diagnosed as showing psychosis during the childhood attendance.

index cases, as compared with 83.3 per cent for those presenting below age 12 and destined to show schizophrenia. The figures are small and statistical analysis is therefore limited, none the less if this were consistent for a larger group it would represent one of the more striking findings.

AFFECTIVE PSYCHOSIS

Seven adults were given a diagnosis of manic-depressive psychosis but only one was also given this diagnosis in childhood. The graph showing age of onset irrespective of symptomatology revealed a sharp 'cut off' for manic-depressive psychosis as compared with other diagnostic groups (Graph 5.1), only one case having presented earlier than the 12/13 age group. This is further supported by the fact that four of the seven had an acute onset (rather than insidious) in childhood.

The older age of onset could not separate those with future affective psychosis from future schizophrenics as the latter presented across the childhood age range. Some difference in the childhood antecedents of affective psychosis and schizophrenia have already been noted as has the difficulty in using these as diagnostic criteria in childhood. From the case notes there was an impression of more intact functioning before onset and a more complete recovery after the initial episode for those with affective psychosis. Again, though, this was not a clear distinction and may have been only a function of the later onset.

The case notes of some contained erudite discussion between eminent psychiatrists without satisfactory conclusion on diagnosis or prognosis and for the majority it seems that the passage of time is essential to permit the distinction between types of psychosis.

DISCUSSION

Several points emerge from this study with regard to childhood antecedents of adult psychosis in this group who showed early disorder. For the most part schizophrenia and affective psychosis were similar clinically but there were differences. Those with future schizophrenia presented more with an insidious onset, a mixture of antisocial and emotional symptoms, poor concentration, specific developmental delays, peer isolation, and incongruous behaviour. Those presenting earlier in childhood were more likely to show incongruous behaviour and developmental delay than those presenting over the age of 12. The children going on to affective psychosis never presented before the age of 11 with anything, were more likely to have an acute onset and an already apparent affective component. However, though a smaller proportion with future schizophrenia presented in this way, the overall larger number meant that almost as many destined to show schizophrenia presented with the same picture as those with future affective psychosis.

With regard to schizophrenic illnesses earlier literature gave a rather confusing picture of the relationship between childhood disorder and adult psychosis (Bower, 1960; Gardener, 1967; Wittman, 1944; Schofield, 1959; Morris *et al.*, 1956), nearly every childhood pattern being linked to adult schizophrenia. However, as Rutter (1978) pointed out, a pattern has emerged that includes symptoms appearing together that more commonly appear discretely in either emotional or conduct disorders together with academic and social difficulties. Rutter commented that the pattern was not sufficiently distinctive to be useful for predictive purposes and certainly there was a marked resemblance here between disorders preceding schizophrenia and those preceding personality disorder. The description of odd or bizarre behaviour did give some distinction between these two groups, appearing in about 60 per cent of the former and 10 per cent of the latter, so that at least some at increased risk for psychosis may be identifiable. A symptom of 'oddness' does itself present problems of definition. Though the use of such terms tends to be discouraged in the Maudsley Hospital, they were none the less used in the notes to describe many of these future psychotic children, whereas detailed descriptions of the behaviour meriting this term were less often available. Kolvin and colleagues (1971) described thought disorder in children, and it is possible that the oddness is a childhood manifestation equivalent to this adult phenomenon, as children are said to show less specific symptoms and to express themselves in actions rather than words.

Differences were found between younger and older children with regard to later schizophrenia, with greater difficulty of diagnosis, developmental delay and more 'odd' behaviour, but whether such early onset cases represent a separate entity could not be clarified here as there was nothing in this study to distinguish the adult disorder from later onset cases. Though the link with developmental delay relates particularly to boys, the finding is of interest, in view of the work of others suggesting an organic basis for schizophrenia presenting early in life (Offord & Cross, 1969).

Affective psychosis was to some extent under-represented in this study with 4.3 per cent of index cases, as compared with 7.8 per cent for all new patients attending the adult department. The numbers are small but, unlike schizophrenia, no adult with affective psychosis presented before the age of 10 with any childhood disturbance. These results are in agreement with those of other authors who have found manic-depressive psychosis to be rare before the mid-teens (Dahl, 1971; Anthony & Scott, 1960). Berg and colleagues (1974a) considered it to be of sufficient rarity to report a single case with onset at the age of 14. As with other conditions the possibilities arise that the morbid processes and manifestations do not occur in childhood, that in childhood the morbid process is symptomless or that the morbid process results in manifestations that differ in childhood from those in adult life. Annell (1969) treated adolescents with Lithium when more classical features of illness were not clearly manifest and quoted other authors also claiming that 'masked' manic depressive illness occurs (van Stockert, 1956). Campbell (1955) described several cases as being manic depressive with onset between ages 6 and 12 years though his criteria seem somewhat uncritical as do those of Esman and colleagues (1983). Hassanyeh and Davison (1980) presented ten cases before the age of 16 but all their cases were aged 12 and 15 and they also noted the difficulty in diagnosis. The results here cannot help to distinguish between no morbid process and morbid process with no manifestations in childhood but they are in keeping with the view that this illness is unlikely to be manifest in either the usual adult form or any other form before the age of 12 years.

10. Conclusions

The study of the natural history of disorder from childhood to adult life is beset with many pitfalls, and the reliance on any one method could easily lead to false conclusions. The use of case notes provides a glimpse of the course of events over a number of years, though the reliability of the data depends on the skill of the contemporary observer. The standard of case-note recording was high, with considerable standardization of history-taking; even so, this is an imprecise tool that limits examination in fine detail. However, reading the full case notes gives an impression of certain patterns over time that are relevant to the understanding of emotional and behavioural disorders, and to their classification.

The first aspect of the study concerns the possibility of identifying children presenting in a psychiatric clinic who are likely to show further disturbance in adult life. Formal diagnosis did not help in this respect, so that it became necessary to look for other criteria on which to group the children and compare index cases and controls. Environmental and social factors helped little more than formal diagnosis and it was only on individual symptoms and duration of attendance that significant differences were found. Irrespective of the outcome at the end of the childhood attendance, index cases attended the children's department for longer than controls. Certain individual symptoms did differ significantly between index and controls, but clear patterns of symptoms were difficult to see for the whole group, particularly when age and sex differences were taken into account.

In the absence of clearly definable patterns, symptom scores and discriminant function analysis were used to further separate the two groups. Symptom scores were on the whole disappointing, perhaps because all children here, including controls, had sufficient disturbance to merit referral on some criteria, most studies using symptom scores as a measure of current disturbance (Glidewell, 1957; Rutter *et al.*, 1970; Shepherd, 1971). Discriminant function analysis was more helpful and confirmed that a significant number of index cases and controls could be separated from each other. Several factors operated in this study to reduce index/control differences, as for example some child controls may have developed adult illness later than the period of time of the study, and others may well have had adult illness but presented elsewhere without reference to the hospital that they attended as a child. The differences that were found are therefore very encouraging for the identification of a high risk group.

The second part of the study concerns the differences in adult disorder depending on whether or not they had been preceded by manifest childhood disorder. There was again remarkably little difference between index cases and adult controls on symptoms or diagnosis. Two points stood out: the raised incidence of personality disorder, and the overall incompetence of the index cases. The latter was reflected in such items as dependence, marriage, divorce, social class, and court record, these findings being very similar to those in the study of Robins (1966). Personality disorder did occur in the control group, and though childhood symptoms may not have been recorded, psychiatric attendance in childhood was, it is to be hoped, less likely to be missed. Re-examination of the case notes gave the impression that the personality-disordered controls were none the less better organized and more competent than those in the index group, and some of the differences in the recorded data are consistent with this.

The third part of the study relates to the general associations between childhood and adult disorder when both have occurred. Many of the findings confirm those of other studies, particularly that of Robins (1966). This is quite important as the study here is probably the closest to a replication study carried out in this country. Continuity of symptoms from childhood to adult life irrespective of diagnosis was one of the strongest findings. Where disorder recurred then symptoms occurring in childhood reappeared. This seemed true of each symptom independently, for example, antisocial behaviour predicted antisocial behaviour whether or not emotional or neurotic symptoms were present.

This is not to say that symptoms did not cluster as some symptoms certainly did. However, the relative independence of symptom continuity appears to have been one of the factors making symptom predictability far better than diagnostic predictability.

Symptom continuity and cluster or syndrome continuity are not the same thing and might co-exist. This can be illustrated by a simple diagram (Diagram 10.1).

Thus, whilst cluster I later gives cluster II and cluster III gives cluster IV, symptom D continues once it occurs. These patterns could be elaborated further, depending on whether D characterizes one of the syndromes and is essential, or whether it may only possibly occur but once it occurs continues to do so. The picture is further complicated by the possible importance and continuity of other coexisting symptoms.

In this study symptoms seemed to behave in this manner both with regard to emotional disorder and to conduct disorder. Obsessions,

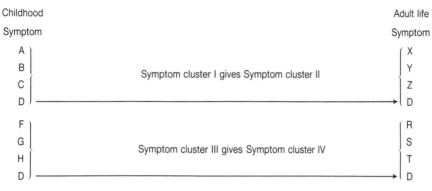

Childhood   Adult life

Symptom   Symptom

A ⎫   ⎧ X
B ⎪   ⎪ Y
C ⎬   Symptom cluster I gives Symptom cluster II   ⎨ Z
D ⎭ ───→ ⎩ D

F ⎫   ⎧ R
G ⎪   ⎪ S
H ⎬   Symptom cluster III gives Symptom cluster IV   ⎨ T
D ⎭ ───→ ⎩ D

Diagram 10.1

depression, antisocial behaviour, and aggression each appeared at times to characterize the disorder, each had their own continuity, but often co-existed in some combination.

The situation appears not unlike that occurring in previous centuries' with regard to the symptomatic and syndromatic classifications that were used for physical disorder. Cough, purulent sputum, and swollen ankles might tend to occur together but do not necessarily relate to a single underlying pathology. Similarly fever for whatever cause may have some constant effects, but may be related to many other syndromes, etc. It would seem that in child psychiatry more weight could be given to the prognostic value of symptoms but that single symptoms would not make a suitable basis for classification except where they can be shown to be the essential and charcterizing feature.

The follow-up data in this study is in general agreement with a distinction between childhood conduct disorder and emotional disorder (Rutter, 1978). The continuities from emotional disorder in childhood to neurotic disorder in adult life and from antisocial behaviour in childhood to antisocial behaviour in adult life seemed fairly constant when each occurred in the absence of the other. The children showing mixed conduct and neurotic disorder show a less certain pattern but overall it seemed that the continuities still held, following their own course rather than being mutually exclusive. For example, in emotionally disordered children it was the absence of antisocial behaviour that predicted its absence in adult life.

There were exceptions to the continuities, none the less, and these may be reviewed briefly here, though in the text some of these are dealt with in different chapters.

Violence or aggression in childhood invariably was followed by adult psychosis or personality disorder, but violence itself might not be present in adult life. There was nothing particular to distinguish those in whom violence apparently diminished. Conduct disorder of all forms was almost invariably followed by adult personality disorder or psychosis but there were two exceptions who later had adult neurotic disorder but functioned well enough not to merit a diagnosis of personality disorder. There seemed to be no distinguishing features in these cases either. Similarly, those children who appeared in court only in childhood and not again in adult life seemed to have little to unify them as a group.

A slightly clearer picture could be seen for the discontinuities in the other direction, that is where antisocial or aggressive behaviour appeared for the first time in adult life. Of the children diagnosed as having only emotional disorder all but four went on to show emotional or neurotic disorder in adult life. Of the four exceptions one later developed psychosis, and the other three developed antisocial personality disorder. The features that they seemed to have in common in childhood were principally dependence, an aversion to school, and in adult life sexual disorders. Hersov (1977b), in reviewing school refusal, only briefly mentioned hostile dependent relationships but did not describe an antisocial outcome. Tyrer and Tyrer (1974) found a link with adult disorder, but as their study used only adults with phobias, anxiety, or depression the type of outcome here could not have been detected. There were also some differences between those who appeared in court for the first time in adult life and those who had previously been to court both as a child and adult. Aggression and organic impairment seemed to characterize the adult-only group, irrespective of diagnosis, and variety and persistence of antisocial behaviour was more characteristic of the child and adult court attenders. There was indeed some indication that when aggressive behaviour appeared for the first time in adult life there was in any case greater likelihood of some form of organic impairment.

Finally, altogether six adults showed violent or antisocial behaviour in adult life without similar behaviour being recorded in childhood. Two of these were diagnosed as having a psychotic disorder as adults. The other four had personality disorders and two had obsessional disorders additionally. In childhood they had a mixture of diagnostic labels, two showed developmental delay, one school refusal and one hysteria. These cases are important as in this study childhood antisocial behaviour constantly preceded antisocial disorder, but did not do so invariably as Robins (1978) suggested.

The study as reported here looked particularly at four different types of disorder with regard to their links and continuities between childhood and adult life, depression, obsessive compulsive disorders, conduct disorder and personality disorder and psychosis.

Several findings emerged in this study concerning depressive disorders. First reactive depression had a course and prognosis different from other emotional or neurotic disorders. Depression was, for example, associated with personality disorder in a way that other emotional disorders were not. The pattern for age of presentation in childhood was a characteristic U shape, and again different from that of other emotional disorders. The term characteristic is used here because no matter how depression was identified, a similar curve for the age distribution in childhood was found. The same pattern had been reported by other authors (Cytryn & Mcknew, 1974; Editorial BMJ, 1971; Rutter, 1972a) and various explanations have been put forward involving differences in exposure to external causes, the development of defence mechanisms, cognitive development, and masking or difference in the manifestation of depressive disorder in childhood. The very persistence of the shape of the curve, particularly when related to adult depression would indicate that whatever the mechanism, the trough in mid childhood was real rather than due to a higher rate of unrecognized depression in this age range.

Secondly, the symptoms of depression showed quite strong continuity into adult life in the index cases, but the clinical diagnosis initially used by the assessors on adult cases was of relatively little value. On this basis depression seemed less common in the index group. Using a computer-generated depressive syndrome based on the work of Pearce (1974), depression appeared to have good continuity into adult life and appeared in index cases in a similar proportion to the adult controls.

The principal reason for the advantage of this syndrome seemed to be that it could be applied irrespective of any other diagnosis made. The continuity found here for both the symptom and the generated syndromes is of considerable importance as there is little evidence from previous studies showing this. Graham (1974, 1981) made a case for a difference between depressive states and other emotional disorders in children and this seems to be supported here. It does not seem surprising to find that depression may be classified in various parts of the WHO classification (Rutter *et al.*, 1975) and it might be reasonable to separate all affective states (other than affective psychosis) into an independent category.

Thirdly there was little evidence to support the presence of any significant number of masked depressions in childhood. With the continuity found it would have been that there would have been much stronger links with other 'masking' childhood symptoms. The depressive syndrome generated from a fixed symptom list in childhood that did not require the mandatory presence of altered mood was not of predictive value for adult depression unless the childhood symptom was present. It could also be seen that for adults with depression the age of childhood presentation irrespective of symptomatology followed the pattern anticipated for overt depression in childhood.

Finally there was support for the view that contact with psychiatrically disturbed parents was pathogenic for depression. This contrasted with the evidence concerning loss of a parent. No clear association could be found between loss of parents by death or separation and later depression, though loss of a parent was found to be pathogenic for personality disorder.

Obsessional disorders stood out as a special case in this study, and the symptom of obsessions would appear to merit more importance in its own right. It was over-represented in the index group, as compared with both child controls and adult controls in spite of being one of the less common symptoms present in either. Irrespective of diagnosis there was very strong symptom continuity and indeed this was one of the few circumstances where the majority of adults with the symptom had previously shown it in childhood. The diagnosis of obsessional disorder showed a similar pattern but with less strong associations. It appeared that this was largely due to the difficulty in selecting a diagnostic label when several major symptoms were present simultaneously, for example, obsessions, phobias, depression, anxiety. The case would be made from this study, that whatever the diagnosis made on other symptoms, if obsessions are present then they should be noted with the diagnostic labels as they would probably be of more value prognostically than nearly anything else. Most emotional disorders of childhood have a good prognosis, and on these grounds alone obsessional disorders would seem 'uneasily' classified in this group.

Many of the findings concerning conduct disorder and personality disorder have already been discussed in connection with the general continuities and discontinuities between childhood and adult life. Robins (1966) noted that though conduct-disordered childen may make satisfactory adjustment, if they do not then adult personality disorder will almost certainly ensue. Delinquency here represented a more severe conduct disorder, and particularly for this group personality disorder was the inevitable outcome, with the exception of a few who developed psychosis.

In spite of all the exceptions one distinction appeared to be that though emotional disorders, for example, arise and fade perhaps to reappear in adult life personality disorder is more of a continuous process affected by various childhood factors including psychiatric disorder. Clearly not all conduct disorders are part of a deviation of personality development, but a childhood diagnostic category or scale that reflected deviant personality development could well have its merits. Greenspan & Lourie (1981) proposed a scheme on these lines for early infancy and childhood that they describe as a 'developmental structuralist' approach to classification. Their system leaves many problems of definition, reliability and validity but perhaps makes an interesting start.

The future personality-disordered subject in this study could be characterized by the following list:

Difficulty in school
Truancy
Histrionic behaviour
Violence (males)
Stealing
Lying
Peer isolation (younger males)
Overdependency (young males)
Separation from or loss of a parent

The classification of personality disorder in adults continues to present problems (Tyrer & Alexander, 1979) and the findings here suggest that course from childhood and severity of dysfunction may be of value in developing some form of satisfactory classification. Control cases did show personality disorder, but there appeared to be differences in the nature of their disorder compared with index cases that were partly reflected in symptomatology. Some of the discontinuities from childhood within the index group also suggested differences in types of personality disorder. When Tyrer and Alexander attempted to define satisfactory groupings for personality disorder they only considered immediate symptoms so that course from childhood could not have been detected as a distinguishing factor.

For psychotic disorders several conclusions could be drawn. Firstly the poor prognosis for psychosis with onset at adolescence is confirmed. Secondly for most of this group it seemed futile to try to distinguish between manic-depressive psychosis and schizophrenia. Steinberg (1977) found no typical cases of manic-depressive psychosis in 500 admissions aged 11–18 and Graham and Rutter (1973) also commented on the difficult differentiation between the two groups of psychosis. In this study it could be seen that where a 'decision' between manic-depressive psychosis and schizophrenia was made, it was likely to be wrong according to subsequent course. It may therefore be better to use a wider term of psychosis and avoid further identification until later. An acute onset was about the only factor that pointed more to manic-depressive psychosis as it was more often the mode of onset for this disorder. Unfortunately as there were far more cases of schizophrenia, an acute onset could not actually help to distinguish between the two types of disorder.

Thirdly adults with schizophrenia presenting before the age of 13 showed a constellation of symptoms. Rutter (1971) noting this pattern from various studies reviewed, did not consider it distinctive enough for predictive purposes.

The pattern seen here included antisocial behaviour, emotional symptoms, peer isolation and developmental delay, bizarre behaviour, and insidious onset. The pattern was very similar to many with future personality disorder, but the description of strangeness and incongruous behaviour distinguished many future 'psychotics'. From the case-note descriptions it seemed that designation of the symptoms as being conduct disorder or emotional disorder was misleading and that in spite of the absences of first-rank symptoms (Schneider, 1959) a similarity could be seen between most index cases destined to develop psychotic illnesses.

The insidious onset may have been the reason why most were not recognized diagnostically until later in life. Kolvin and colleagues (Kolvin *et al.*, 1971) reviewed criteria for schizophrenia in childhood and included thought disorder, which could equate with the puzzling bizarreness in the childen in this study. Kolvin also commented, quoting Fish, that a prolonged case is easier to diagnose than an acute case. The evidence here suggests the reverse in that most acute cases were identified as psychotic and this was confirmed by course into adult life.

There were a number of differences between psychosis commencing before and after the age of 13. The younger cases were harder to identify as psychotic, were more likely to have an insidious onset, and showed more organic and developmental problems. Though not conclusive, the presence of younger onset cases in the controls also suggested a slightly better prognosis than adolescent onset cases. Though no differences could be found in the adult disorder in this study between the younger and older onset cases it is possible that they represent different types of disorder within the schizophrenic group.

The study as a whole gives a general impression of those people with disorder both in childhood and adult life. Several patterns seemed to be present. Many of the index cases were individuals who were incompetent or incapacitated in some way and who were at the same time in an unsupportive environment. It was of note that the incompetence was even apparent in comparison with controls receiving the same diagnosis. For some, disorder in adult life seemed relatively unrelated to the childhood disorder except that symptoms, once established in childhood, tended to recur irrespective of the adult diagnosis. Other conditions, for example psychotic disorder and obsessional disorders seemed to arise in childhood and more or less continue as the same into adult life, albeit with 'well' intervals. Whichever of these patterns applied, nearly all of the index cases seemed to be people with more pervasive disorder than the adult controls.

Classification of childhood disorders continues to present major difficulties and at present there is no really satisfactory system. The WHO study (Rutter *et al.*, 1969, 1975) has gone a long way to providing a useful system that can aid communication and research, but its largely empirical basis with operational definitions causes frequent forced choices.

The findings in this study indicate some modifications in classification of childhood disorder. Perhaps the most striking general observation was the relative independence of different types of symptoms, and the difficulties created by a forced choice on a single axis. Individual coexisting symptoms would seem to merit more weight and affective states might even be separately classified. This would almost certainly result in a more complex sytem, but human behaviour is complex and it seems unlikely that all aspects of dysfunction could be classified in the same manner.

References

List includes additional references consulted but not quoted in the text.

Abe, K. (1972). Phobias and nervous symptoms in childhood and maturity. *British J. Psychiat.*, **120**, 275

Adams, P. (1973). *Obsessive children: A Sociopsychiatric Study.* Brunner/Mazel, New York.

Agras, K. (1959). Relationship of school refusal to depression. *Amer. J. Psychiat.*, **116**, 533.

Ainsworth, M. D. (1966). In *Deprivation of Maternal Care: A Reassessment of its Effects.* Schocken Books, New York.

Angst, J. (1975). Personal communication.

——, Banstrup, P., Groff, P., Hippius, N., Polding, W. & Weiss, P. (1973). Course of monopolar depression and bipolar psychosis. *Psychiat., Neurol., Neurochir.*, **76**, 489.

Annell, A. (1969). Lithium in treatment of children and adolescents. *Acta Psychiat., Scand., Supp.* **207**, 19.

Annesley, P. T. (1961). Psychiatric illness in adolescence: Presentation and prognosis. *J. Ment. Sci.*, **107**, 268–78.

Anthony, E. J. (1967). Psychoneurotic disorders of childhood. In *A Comprehensive Textbook of Psychiatry*, (eds. Freedman, A. & Kaplan, H.) pp. 1387–406. Williams & Wilkins, Baltimore.

——, & Scott, P. (1960). Manic-depressive psychosis in childhood. *J. Child Psychol. Psychiat.*, **1**, 53.

Apley, J. (1959). *The Child with Abdominal Pain.* Blackwell, Oxford.

—— (1968). Paediatrics and child psychiatry in Great Britain. In *Foundations of Child Psychiatry*, (ed. Miller, E.) pp. 29–42. Pergamon, Oxford.

Arnold, L. E. & Smelzer, D. J. (1974). Behaviour check list factor analysis for children and adolescents. *Arch. Gen. Psychiat.*, **30**, 799.

August, G. J., Stewart, M. A. & Holmes, C. S. (1983). A four-year follow-up of hyperactive boys with and without conduct disorder. *Brit. J. Psychiat.* **143**, 192–5.

Baddeley, R. (1622). *The Boy of Bilson.* Barrett, London.

Baldwin, J. A. (1968). Psychiatric illness from birth to maturity: An epidemiological study. *Acta Psychiat. Scand.*, **44**, 313.

Barraclough, B. M. & Bunch, J. (1973). Accuracy in dating parent deaths: Recollected dates compared with death certificate dates. *Brit. J. Psychiat.*, **123**, 573.

Barry, M. (1936). A study of bereavement: An approach to problems in mental disease. *J. Abn. Soc. Psychol.*, **30**, 431.

Berg, I., Hullin, R., Allsopp, M., O'Brien, P. & Macdonald, R. (1974a). Bipolar manic-depressive psychosis in early adolescence: A case report. *Brit. J. Psychiat.*, **125**, 416.

——, Marks, I., McClure, R. & Lipsedge, M. (1974b). School phobia and agrophobia. *Psychol. Med.*, **4**, 428.

Berger, M., Yule, W. & Rutter, M. (1975). Attainment and adjustment in two geographic areas. II: Prevalence of specific reading retardation. *Brit. J. Psychiat.,* **126**, 510.

Birtchnell, J. (1971). Social class, parental social class and social mobility in psychiatric patients. *Path. Med.,* **1**, 209.

Bower, E. M. (1960). School characteristics of male adolescents who later develop schizophrenia. *Amer. J. Orthopsychiat.,* **30**, 712.

Bowlby, J. (1951). Maternal care and mental health. *Bull. World Health Organization,* **3**, 355.

——, (1961). Process of mourning. *Int. J. Psychoanal.,* **42**, 317.

——, Ainsworth, M., Boston, M. & Rosenbluth, D. (1956). Effects of mother child separation: a follow-up study. *Brit. J. Med. Psychol.,* **29**, 211.

Bradley, P. E., Wakefield, J. A., Byong-Hee, L. Y., Doughtie, E. B., Cox, J. A. & Kraft, I. A. (1974). Parental MMPI and certain pathological behaviour in children. *J. Clin. Psychol.,* **30**, 379.

Brigham, A. (1839). *Remarks on the influence of mental cultivation and mental excitement upon health,* 4th ed. Whittaker, London.

Brill, N. Q. & Liston, E. H. (1966). Parental loss in adults with emotional disorders. *Arch. Gen. Psychiat.,* **14**, 307.

Bronson, W. C. (1967). Adult derivatives of emotional expressiveness and reactivity control. Developmental continuities from childhood. *Child. Dev.,* **38**, 801.

Brown, F. (1961). Depression and childhood bereavement. *J. Ment. Sci.,* **107**, 754.

Brown, F. (1966). Childhood bereavement and subsequent psychiatric disorder. *Brit. J. Psychiat.,* **112**, 1035.

Brown, F., Epps, P. & McGlashan, A. (1961). Neurotic and immediate effects of orphanhood. *Proceedings of 3rd World Congress of Psychiatry.* McGill University Press, Montreal.

Brown, G. W. & Harris, T. (1978). *Social origins of depression. A study of psychiatric disorder in women.* Tavistock Pub., London.

Burt, C. (1925). *The young delinquent.* University of London Press.

—— (1937). The subnormal school child. Vol. II. *The Backward Child,* University of London Press.

Burton, R. (1628). The Anatomy of Melancholy. 3rd ed. Henry Cripps, Oxford.

Cameron, K. (1955). Diagnostic categories in child psychiatry. *Brit. J. med. Psychol.* **28**, 67.

Campbell, J. D. (1955). Manic depressive illness in children. *J. Amer. Med. Assoc.* **158**, 154.

Carizio, N. (1968). Stability of deviant behaviour in children through time. *Mental Hyg.,* **52**, 288.

Ceriboglu, R. J., Sumer, E. & Polvan, O. (1972). Etiology and pathogenesis of depression in Turkish children. In *Depressive States in Childhood and Adolescence,* (ed. Annell, A.) pp. 133–136. Almquist & Wiksell, Stockholm.

Chess, S., Thomas, A. & Birch, H. (1966). Distortion in developmental reporting made by parents of behaviourally disturbed children. *J. Amer. Acad. Child Psychiat.,* **5(2)**, 226.

Classification of Occupations (1970). Office of Population Censuses and Surveys. HMSO, London.

Clayton, P. A. (1965). Affective disorders: Mania. *Compr. Psychiat.*, **6**, 313.

Cloninger, C. R., Reich, J. & Guze, S. B. (1975). The multifactorial model of disease transmission: II. Sex differences in familial transmission of sociopathy. *Brit. J. Psychiat.* **127**, 11–22.

Collins, L. F. & Maxwell, A. E. (1962). A factor analysis of some child psychiatric clinical data. *J. Ment. Sci.,* **108**, 274.

Conners, C. K. (1976). Classification and treatment of childhood depression and depressive equivalents. In *Depression: Behavioural, Diagnostic and Treatment and Concepts,* (ed. Gallant, J. M. & Simpson, G. M.) pp. 181–204. Spectrum Pub, New York.

Coolidge, S. C., Botlie, R. D. & Feeney, B. (1964). A 10-year follow-up study of 66 school phobic children. *Amer. J. Orthopsychiat.*, **34**, 675.

Craig, M. M. & Glick, S. J. (1963a). Ten years experience with the Glueck Social Prediction Table. *Crime & Delinquency,* **9**, 244.

Creak, E. M. (1962). A Letter. *Nervous Child,* **9**, 317.

Criminal Statistics England and Wales (1973) HMSO, London.

Crook, T. & Elliot, J. (1980). Parental death during childhood and adult depression: A critical review of the literature. *Psychol. Bull.,* **87**, (**2**), 252.

——, Raskin, A. & Elliot, J. (1981). Parent–child relationships and adult depression. *Child Dev.,* **52** (**3**), 950–7.

Crowe, T. J., Johnstone, E. C., Owen, F. (1979). Research on schizophrenia. In *Recent Advances in Clinical Psychiatry,* No 3, (ed. Granville-Grossman, K.) pp. 1–36. Churchill Livingstone, Edinburgh.

Cullen (1784). *The First Lines in the Practice of Physic.* Edinburgh: Elliot. (Cited by Hunter & McAlpine, 1963.)

Cytryn, L. & McKnew, D. H. (1972). Proposed classification of childhood depression. *Amer. J. Psychiat.,* **129** (**2**), 149–55.

—— —— (1974). Factors influencing the changing clinical expression of the depressive process in children. *Amer. J. Psychiat.* **131**, 879.

Dahl, V. (1971). A follow-up study of child psychiatric clientele with specific regard to manic depressive psychosis. *Proceedings of 4th U.E.P. Congress, Stockholm,* pp. 534–41. Almquist & Wiksell, Stockholm.

Davie, R., Butler, N. & Goldstein, H. (1972). *From Birth to Seven. Studies in Child Development.* Longman in association with National Children's Bureau, London.

Dibble, E. & Cohen, D. J. (1974). Instrument for measuring children's competence and parental style. *Arch. Gen. Psychiat.,* **30**, 805.

Dohrenwend, B. S. & Dohrenwend, B. P. (1972). Social class and relation of remote to recent stressors. In *Life History Research in Psychopathology,* (eds. Roff, M., Robins, L. N. & Pollock, M.) vol. 2, pp. 170–85. University of Minnesota Press, Minneapolis.

Douglas, J. W. B. (1966). Progress of nervous and troublesome children. *Brit. J. Psychiat.,* **112**, 1115.

—— & Mulligan, D. G. (1961). Emotional adjustment and educational achievement. The preliminary results of a longitudinal study of a national sample of children. *Proc. Roy. Soc. Med.,* **54**, 885.

Dreger, R. N. (1964). A progress report of a factor analysis approach to classification in child psychiatry. *Amer. Psych. Ass. Psych. Report.*, **18**, 22.

Drotar, D. (1974). Concern over categorization of depression in children. *J. Pediat.* **85**, 290.

Earle, A. M. & Earle, B. V. (1961). Early maternal deprivation and later psychiatric illness. *Amer. J. Orthopsychiat.,* **31**, 181.

Eastgate, J. & Gilmore, L. (1984). Long term outcome of depressed children: A follow up study. *Dev. Med. Child. Neurol,* **26** (**1**), 68–80.

Editorial B.M.J. (1971). Depressive illness in childhood. *Brit. Med. J.,* **1**, 2.

Eggers, C. (1978). Course and prognosis of childhood schizophrenia. *J. Autism Child. Schiz.,* **8** (**1**), 21–36.

Esman, A. H., Hertzig, M. & Aarons, S. (1983). Juvenile manic-depressive illness: A longitudinal perspective. *J. Amer. Acad. Child Psychiat.,* **22** (**3**), 302–4.

Eysenck, H. J. & Prell, D. B. (1951). The inheritance of neuroticism. An experimental study. *J. Ment. Sci.,* **97**, 441.

Fish, B. (1960). Involvement of the central nervous system in infants with schizophrenia. *Arch. Neurol.,* **2**, 115–21.

Frazee, H. E. (1953). Children who later become schizophrenic. *Smith Coll. Stud. Soc. Work,* **23**, 125.

Freeman, T. (1974). Childhood psychopathology and psychotic phenomena in adults. *Brit. J. Psychiat.,* **124**, 556.

Freud, S. (1901). *The Psychopathology of Everyday Life.* Reprinted 1966. Benn, London.

—— (1905). *Three Essays on the Theory of Sexuality.* (English translation by J. Strachey, 1949). *Int. Psychoanal. Lib.,* No. 57. Hogarth Press, London.

—— (1933). *New Introductory Lectures on Psychoanalysis.* 7th imp. 1967. *Int. Psychoanal. Lib.* No. 24, Hogarth Press, London.

Frommer, E. A. (1968). Depressive disorders in childhood. In *Recent Developments in Affective Disorders,* (ed. Coppen, A. & Walk, A.) *Brit. J. Psychiat.,* Spec. Pub. No. 2. pp. 117–36. Headley Brothers, Ashford, Kent.

—— & Cottom, D. (1970). Undiagnosed abdominal pain. *Brit. Med. J.,* **4**, 113.

——, Mendelson, W. B. & Reid, M. A. (1972). Differential diagnosis of disorder in preschool children. *Brit. J. Psychiat.,* **121**, 71.

—— & O'Shea, G. (1973). The importance of childhood experience in relation to problems of marriage and family building. *Brit. J. Psychiat.,* **123**, 157.

GAP Report (1966). *Psychopathological Disorders in Childhood. Theoretical Considerations and a Proposed Classification Group for the Advancement of Psychiatry.* Vol. VI, Report 62, New York: GAP Publications.

Gardener, G. G. (1967). The relationship between childhood neurotic symptomatology in later schizophrenia in males and females. *J. Nerv. Ment. Dis.,* **144**, 97.

Garmezy, N. (1974). Children at risk: the search for the antecedents of schizophrenia. Part I: Conceptual models and research methods. *Schiz. Bull.,* **8**, 13–90.

Gibbens, T. C. N. (1963). The effects of physical ill-health in adolescent delinquency. *Proc. Roy. Soc. Med.,* **56**, 1086.

Glidewell, J. C., Mensh, I. M. & Gilden, M. C. (1957). Behavioural symptoms in children and degree of sickness. *Amer. J. Psychiat.,* **114**, 47.

Glossary of mental disorders. (1968). Studies on medical and population subjects No 22. HMSO, London.

Gluck, I. & Wrenn, M. (1959). Contributions to the understanding of disturbances of mothering. *Brit. J. Med. Psychol.,* **32**, 171.

Glueck, S & Glueck E. T. (1940). *Juvenile Delinquents Grown Up.* Commonwealth Fund, New York.

—— & —— (1950). *Unravelling Juvenile Delinquency.* Harvard University Press, Boston.

Graham, P. (1974). Depression in prepubertal children. *Dev. Med. Child Neurol.,* **16**, 340.

—— (1981). Depressive disorders in childhood: A reconsideration. *Acta Paedopsychiat.,* **46**, 285.

——, Rutter, M. & George, S. (1973). Temperamental characteristics as predictors of behaviour disorders in children. *Amer. J. Orthopsychiat.,* **12**, 136.

—— & —— (1973). Psychiatric disorder in the young adolescent: A follow-up study. *Proc. Roy. Soc. Med.,* **66**, 1226.

Granville-Grossman, K. (1966). Early bereavement and schizophrenia. *Brit. J. Psychiat.,* **112**, 1027.

Greenhill, L. L. & Shopsin, B. (1979). Survey of mental disorders in the children of patients with affective disorders. In *Genetic Aspects of Affective Illness* (eds. Mendlewicz, J. & Shopsin, B.), pp. 75–92. S. P. Medical & Scientific Books, New York.

Greenspan, S. & Lourie, K. S. (1981). Developmental structuralist approach to the classification of adaptive and pathological personality organization: Infancy and childhood. *Amer. J. Psychiat.,* **138 (b)**, 725.

Gregory, I. (1965). Anterospective data following childhood loss of a parent. *Arch. Gen. Psychiat.* **13**, 99.

Gross, M. & Wilson, W. C. (1974). *Minimal Brain Dysfunction.* Brunner/Mazel, New York.

Haley, E. (1973). Strategic therapy when the child is the presenting problem. *J. Amer. Acad. Child Psychiat.,* **12**, 641.

Hagnell, O. (1966). *A prospective study of the incidence of mental disorders.* Svenska Bokförlaget, Norstedts, Stockholm.

Hambert, G. & Akesson, H. O. (1973). A sociopsychiatric follow-up study of two hundred breech-born children. *Acta Psychiat. Scand.,* **49**, 264.

Hanson, D. R., Gottesman, I. I. & Heston, L. L. (1976). Some possible childhood indicators of adult schizophrenia inferred from children of schizophrenics. *Brit. J. Psychiat.,* **129**, 142–54.

Hare, E. (1971). The Bethlem Royal and the Maudsley Hospital Triennial Statistical Report. Years 1967–1969. Bethlem Royal Hospital and Maudsley Hospital, London.

Hare, E. N., Price, J. S. & Slater, E. (1972). Parental social class in psychiatric patients. *Brit. J. Psychiat.,* **121**, 515.

Hassanyeh, F. & Davison, K. (1980). Bipolar affective psychosis before age 16. *Brit. J. Psychiat.,* **137**, 530.

Henderson, D. K. (1939). *Psychopathic States.* Norton, New York.

Hersov, L. (1960a). Persistent non-attendance at school. *J. Child Psychiat.,* **1**, 130.

—— (1960b). Refusal to go to school. *J. Child Psychiat.,* **1**, 137.

—— (1977a). Emotional disorders. In *Child Psychiatry: Modern Approaches,* (eds. Rutter, M. & Hersov, L.) pp. 428–54. Blackwell Scientific Publications, Oxford.

—— (1977b). School Refusal. (Ibid). pp. 455–86.

Hewitt, L. & Jenkins, R. (1946). *Fundamental Patterns of Maladjustment. The Dynamics of their Origin.* State of Illinois: Michigan Child Guidance Institute.

Hollingworth, C. E., Tanguay, P. E., Grossman, L. & Pabst, P. (1980). Long term outcome of obsessive-compulsive disorder in childhood *J. Amer. Acad. Child Psychiat.*, **19**, 134–44.

Huessy, H. R., Marshall, C. D. & Gandron, R. (1973). Five hundred children followed from Grade 2 through Grade 5 for prevalence of behavioural disorder. *Acta Pedopsychiat.*, **39**, Fasc. 11, 277.

Huffman, P. W. (1954). Prodromal Behaviour Patterns in Mental Illness. Dept. of Mental Welfare, State of Illinois, Minnesota.

Hunter, R. & McAlpine, I. (1963). *Three Hundred Years of Psychiatry 1535–1860*. Oxford University Press, London.

Jenkins, R. G. & Glickman, S. (1946). Common syndromes in child psychiatric deviant behaviour traits. *Amer. J. Orthopsychiat.*, **16**, 244.

Jenkins, R. L. (1964). Diagnosis, dynamics and treatment in child psychiatry. *Amer. Psychiat. Ass. Res. Report.* **18**, 91.

—— (1966). Psychiatric syndromes in children and their relationship to family background. *Amer. J. Orthopsychiat.*, **36**, 450.

Johnson, J. (1836). *The Economy of Health or The Stream of Human Life from the Cradle to the Grave.* S. Highley. London.

Jones, F. H. (1974). A 4-year follow-up of vulnerable adolescents. *J. Nerv. Ment. Dis.*, **159**(i), 20.

Judd, L. L. (1965). Obsessive compulsive neurosis in children. *Arch. Gen. Psychiat.*, **12**, 136.

Jung, C. G. (1954). *The Development of the Personality.* Routledge & Kegan Paul, London.

Kagan, J. & Moss, H. (1960). The stability of passive and dependent behaviour from childhood through adulthood. *Child Dev.*, **31**, 577.

Kanner, L. (1959). Trends in child psychiatry. *J. Ment. Sci.*, **105**, 581.

—— (1972). *Child Psychiatry.* 4th ed. Thomas, Springfield, Illinois.

Kashani, J. H., Husain, A., Shekim, W. O., Hodges, K. K., Cytryn, L. & McKnew, D. H. (1981). Current perspectives in childhood depression: An overview. *Amer. J. Psychiat.*, **138**, 143.

Kendell, R. E. (1968). The problem of classification. In *Recent Developments in Affective Disorders* (eds. Coppen, A. & Walk, A.). Royal Medico-Psychological Association. Special Pub. **2**. pp. 15–26. Headley Brothers, Ashford, Kent.

—— (1970). The clinical distinctions between psychotic and neurotic depression, *Brit. J. Psychiat.*, **117**, 257.

Kerr, T. A., Roth, M., Shapiro, K. & Gurney, C. (1972). The assessment and prediction of outcome in affective disorders. *Brit. J. Psychiat.*, **121**, 167.

Kiloh, L. G. & Garside, R. G. (1963). The independence of neurotic depression and endogenous depression. *Brit. J. Psychiat.*, **109**, 451.

Klerman, G. L. (1976). Age and clinical depression. Today's youth in the twenty-first century. *Gerontol.*, **31**, 318.

Kolvin, I., Ounsted, C., Humphrey, M. & McNay, A. (1971). The phenomenology of childhood psychoses. *Brit. J. Psychiat.*, **118**, 385.

—— & Nicol, A. R. (1979). Child psychiatry. In *Recent Advances in Clinical Psychiatry*, (ed. Granville-Grossman, K.), No. 3, pp. 297–332. Churchill Livingstone, London.

Kovacs, M., Feinberg, T. L., Crouse-Novak, M. A., Palauskas, S. L. & Finklestein, R. (1984). Depressive disorders in children. *Arch. Gen. Psychiat.* **41** (3), 229–37.

Kraepelin, E. (1919). *Dementia Praecox and Paraphrenia.* Livingstone, Edinburgh.

Kraupl-Taylor, F. (1966). *Psychopathology. Its Causes and Symptoms.* Butterworths, London.

Kringlen, E. (1965). Obsessional neurotics: Long-term follow-up. *Brit. J. Psychiat.,* **111**, 709.

Kupfer, D. J., Defoe, T. P. & Koral, J. (1975). Relationship of certain childhood traits to adult psychiatric disorders. *Amer. J. Orthopsychiat.,* **45 (i)**, 74.

Langford, W. S. (1964). Reflections on classification in child psychiatry as related to the activity of the Committee on Child Psychiatry of the Group for the Advancement of Psychiatry. *Amer. Psychiat. Ass. Res. Report,* **18**, 1. GAP Publications, New York.

Lapouse, R. & Monk, M. A. (1958). Epidemiological study of behavioural characteristics in children. *Amer. J. Pub. Health.,* **48**, 1134.

Lavik, A. (1973). The classification problem in child and adolescent psychiatry. *Acta Psychiat. Scand.,* **49**, 131.

Lebovitz, P. S. (1972). Feminine behaviour in boys. Aspects of outcome. *Amer. J. Psychiat.,* **128**, 10.

Leibman, R., Minuchin, S. & Baher, L. (1974). The use of family therapy in the treatment of intractable asthma. *Amer. J. Psychiat.,* **131**, 535.

Lesse, S. (1974). Depression masked by acting out behaviour. *Amer. J. Psychother.,* **28**, 352.

Lewine, R. R. J., Watt, N. F., Prentky, R. A. & Fryer, J. H. (1980). Childhood social competence in functionally disordered psychiatric patients and in normals. *J. Abn. Psychol.,* **89 (2)**, 132–8.

Lewis, W. W. (1965). Continuity and intervention in emotional disturbance. A review. *Except. Child.,* **31**, 465.

Ling, W., Oftedal, G. & Weinberg, W. (1970). Depressive illness in children presenting as severe headache. *Amer. J. Dis. Child.,* **120**, 122.

Liss, J. L., Wolner, A. & Robins, E. (1973). Personality disorder. Part I: Record study. *Brit. J. Psychiat.,* **123**, 685.

Livson, N. & Peskin, N. (1967). Prediction of adult psychological health in a longitudinal study. *J. Abn. Psychol.,* **72**, 509.

Lo, W. H. (1967). A follow-up study of obsessive compulsive neurotics in Hong Kong. *Brit. J. Psychiat.,* **113**, 823.

—— (1973). A note on a follow-up study of childhood neurosis and behaviour disorder. *J. Child Psychol. Psychiat,* **14**, 147.

Locke, J. (1709). *Some Thoughts concerning Education.* Sixth ed. A. & J. Churchill, London.

Lyon, M. E. & Plomin, R. (1981). The measurement of temperament using parental scales. *J. Child. Psychol. Psychiat.,* **22**, 47.

Macfarlane, J. W., Allen, L. & Hoznik, M. P. (1954). *A Developmental Study of the Behavioural Problem of Normal Children between 21 Months and 14 Years.* University of California Press. Berkeley and Los Angeles.

Makita, K. (1974). The rarity of depression in childhood. *Acta Paedopsychiat.,* **40**, 37.

Malmivaara, K., Keinanen, E. & Saarelma, M. (1975). Factors affecting child psychiatric hospital care and its immediate results. *Psychiat. Fennica.,* 225–38.

Mapother, E. (1926). Discussion on manic depressive psychosis. *Brit. Med. J.* **2.**, 872–6.

Marks, I. N. (1973). Research in neurosis. A selective review. I. Causes and courses. *Psychol. Med.,* **3**, 436.

—— & Gelder, M. G. (1966). Different ages of onset or varieties of phobias. *Amer. J. Psychiat.,* **123**, 218.

Masterson, J. F. (1958). Prognosis in adolescent disorders. *Amer. J. Psychiat.,* **114**, 1097.

—— (1967). The symptomatic adolescent five years later. *Amer. J. Psychiat.,* **123**, 1338.

Mattisson, M., Hawkins, J. W. & Seese, L. R. (1967). Child psychiatric emergencies: Clinical characteristics and follow-up results. *Arch. Gen. Psychiat.,* **17**, 584.

McDevitt, S. C. & Casey, W. B. (1978). The measurement of temperament in 3–7 year old children. *J. Child Psychol. Psychiat.,* **19**, 245.

Medinnus, G. R. & Johnson, R. C. (1969). *Child and Adolescent Psychology. Behaviour and Development.* Wiley, New York.

Mellsopp, G. W. (1972). Psychiatric patients seen as children and adults. Childhood predictors of adult illness. *J. Child Psychol. Psychiat.,* **13**, 91.

—— (1973). Adult psychiatric patients on whom information was recorded during childhood. *Brit. J. Psychiat.,* **123**, 703.

Mendlewicz, J. & Klotz, J. (1974). Primary enuresis and affective illness. *Lancet,* **1**, 733.

Michaels, J. S. (1955). Disorder of character. *Persistent enuresis, juvenile delinquency and psychopathic personality.* Thomas, Springfield, Illinois.

Moore, T., Hindley, C. B. & Falkner, F. (1954). Longitudinal research in child development and some of its problems. *Brit. Med. J.,* **2**, 1132.

Morris, H., Soroker, E. & Burriss, G. (1954). A follow-up study of shy withdrawn children. Valuation of late adjustment. *Amer. J. Orthopsychiat.,* **24**, 743.

——, Escoll, P. S. & Wexler, R. (1956). Aggressive behaviour disturbance of childhood. A follow-up study. *Amer. J. Psychiat.,* **112**, 991.

Mulligan, G., Douglas, J. W. B., Hammond, W. A. & Tizard, J. (1963). Delinquency and symptoms of maladjustment. The findings of a longitudinal study. *Proc. Roy Soc. Med.,* **56**, 1083.

Murray, L. G. & Blackburn, I. M. (1974). Personality differences in patients with depressive illness and anxiety neurosis. *Acta Psychiat. Scand.,* **50**, 183.

Myers, J. K., Lindenthal, J. & Pepper, M. (1972). Life events and mental status—a longitudinal study. *J. Health Soc. Behav.* **13**, 398.

Offord, D. R. & Cross, L. (1969). Behavioural antecedents of adult schizophrenia. *Arch. Gen. Psychiat.,* **21**, 267.

—— & —— (1971). Adult schizophrenia with scholastic failure or low IQ in childhood. *Arch. Gen. Pschiat.,* **24**, 431.

O'Neal, P. & Robins, L. (1958). The relations of childhood behavioural problems to adult psychiatric states. A 30-year follow-up study of 150 subjects. *Amer. J. Psychiat.,* **114**, 961.

——, ——, King, L. J. & Schaefer, J. (1962). Parental deviance and the genesis of sociopathic personality. *Amer. J. Psychiat.,* **118**, 1114.

Ovenstone, I. M. K. & Kreitman, M. (1974). Two syndromes of suicide. *Brit. J. Psychiat.,* **124**, 336.

Parkinson, J. (1807). *Observations on the Excessive Indulgence of Children, particularly intended to show its Injurious Effects on their Health and the Difficulties it occasions in their treatment during Sickness.* Symonds, London.

Pasamanick, B. C., Rogers, M. & Lilenfield, A. (1956). Pregnancy experience and the development of behavioural disorders in children. *Amer. J. Psychiat.,* **112,** 613.

Paykel, E. S. & Prussoff, B. A. (1977). Typologies of disturbed behaviour in human psychopharmacology. Problems and possibilities. In *Neurotransmission and Disturbed Behaviour* (eds. Van Praag, H. M. & Brunnels, J.) pp. 188–288. Bohn, Schelemu & Holkema, Utrecht.

—— & Rowan, F. R. (1979). Affective disorders. In *Recent Advances in Clinical Psychiatry,* (ed. Granville-Grossman, K.) pp. 37–90. Churchill Livingstone, Edinburgh.

Pearce, J. B. (1974). Childhood Depression. MPhil. Thesis, University of London.

Pearce, J. (1977). Depressive disorder in childhood. Annotation. *J. Child Psychol. Psychiat.,* **18,** 79.

Perris, C. (1966). A study of bipolar and unipolar recurrent depressive psychosis. *Acta Psychiat. Scand.,* Supp. **194.**

Phillips, L. (1953). Case history data and prognosis and schizophrenia. *J. Nerv. Ment. Dis.,* **117,** 515.

Pitts, F. N., Meyer, J., Brooks, M. & Winokur, G. (1965). Adult psychiatric illness assessed for childhood parental loss and psychiatric illness in family members. *Amer. J. Psychiat.,* **108,** 685.

Pollitt, J. D. (1957). Natural history of obsessional neurosis. *Brit. Med. J.,* **i,** 194.

Post, F. (1965). *The Clinical Psychiatry of Late Life.* Pergamon Press, Oxford.

Poznanski, E. (1980). Childhood depression: The outcome. *Acta Paedopsychiat.,* **46,** 297.

Pringle, M. L. K., Butler, N. R. & Davie, R. (1966). *11,000 Seven-Year-Olds.* Longman, London.

Pritchard, M. & Graham, P. (1966). An investigation of patients who have attended both the child and adult departments of the same psychiatric hospital. *Brit. J. Psychiat.,* **112,** 603.

Puig-Antich, J. & Gittelman, R. (1982). Depression in childhood and adolescence. In *Handbook of Affective Disorders,* (ed. Paykel, E. S.) pp. 379–92. Churchill Livingstone, Edinburgh.

Quitkin, F., Rifkin, A. & Klein, D. F. (1976). Neurological soft signs in schizophrenia and character disorders. *Arch. Gen. Psychiat.,* **33,** 845–53.

Rawnsley, K. (1968). Epidemiology of affective disorders. In *Recent Developments in Affective Disorders,* (eds. Coppen A. & Walk A.) Royal Medico-Psychological Association, Special Publ. 2. pp. 27–36. Headley Brothers, Ashford, Kent.

Rees, J. R. (1939). Sexual difficulties in children. In *A Survey of Child Psychiatry,* (ed. Gordon, P. G.) pp. 246–56. Child Guidance Council, Oxford University Press, London.

Remschmidt, H., Brechtel, B. & Mewe, F. (1973). Zum Krankheitsverlauf und zur Persönlichkeitsstruktur von Kindern und Jugendlichen mit endogen-phasischen Psychosen und reactiven Depressionen. *Acta Paedopsychiat. (Basel),* **40,** 2–17.

Robins, L. (1966). *Deviant Children Grown Up.* Williams & Wilkins, Baltimore.

—— (1974). Childhood and adult psychiatric illness. *Brit. J. Psychiat.,* **124,** 505.

—— (1978). Sturdy predictors of adult antisocial behaviour: Replications from longitudinal studies. *Psychol. Med.,* **8**, 611

—— (1979). Follow-up studies. In *Psychopathological Disorders of Childhood,* (ed. Quay, H. C. & Werry, J. S.) pp. 414–50. Wiley, New York.

Robinson, B. H. (1951). Follow-up of cases after 20 years. 9th Child Guidance Interclinic Conference, pp. 27–37. National Association for Mental Health, London.

Rodriguez, A., Rodriguez, M. & Eisenberg, L. (1959). The outcome of school phobia. *Amer. J. Psychiat.,* **116**, 540.

Roff, M. (1974). Childhood antecedents of adult neurosis, severe bad conduct and psychological health. In *Life History Research in Psychopathology,* (eds. Ricks, D. F., Thomas, A. & Rolf, M.) *Vol. 3,* pp. 131–62. University of Minnesota Press, Minneapolis.

Rolf, J. E. & Garmezy, N. (1974). The school performance of children vulnerable to behavioural pathology. In *Life History Research in Psychopathology,* (eds. Ricks, D. F., Thomas, A. & Rolf, M.) *Vol. 3,* pp. 87–107. University of Minnesota Press, Minneapolis.

Roth, M. (1972). Studies in the classification of affective disorders: The relationship between anxiety states and depressive illness. *Brit. J. Psychiat.,* **121**, 147.

Russell, A. T., Cantwell, D. P., Mattison, K. & Will, C. (1979). A comparison of DSM II and DSM III in the diagnosis of childhood psychiatric disorders. III. Multiaxial features. *Arch. Gen. Psychiat.,* **36**, 1223.

Rutter, M. (1964). Intelligence and childhood psychiatric disorder. *Brit. J. Soc. Clin. Psychol.,* **3**, 120–9.

—— (1965). Classification and categorization in child psychiatry. *J. Child Psychol. Psychiat,* **6**, 71.

—— (1966). *Children of Sick Parents: An Environmental and Psychiatric Study.* Maudsley Monogr. 16. Institute of Psychiatry, Oxford University Press, London.

—— (1970a). Autistic children: Infancy to adulthood. *Seminars in Psychiatry,* **2**, 435–58.

—— (1970b). Psychosocial disorders in childhood and outcome in adult life. *J. Roy. Coll. Phys.,* **4**, 211.

—— (1971). Parent–child separation: Psychological effects on the children. *J. Child Psychol. Psychiat.,* **12**, 233.

—— (1972a). Relationship between child and adult psychiatric disorders: Some research considerations. *Acta Psychiat. Scand,* **48**, 3–21.

—— (1972b) *Maternal Deprivation Reassessed.* Penguin, Harmondsworth.

—— (1972c). Childhood schizophrenia reconsidered. *J. Aut. Child. Schiz.,* **2** (4), 315.

—— (1973). Why are London children so disturbed? *Proc. Roy. Soc. Med.,* **66**, 1221.

—— (1977a). Surveys to answer questions: Some methodological considerations. In *Epidemiological Approaches in Child Psychiatry,* (ed. Graham, P.) pp. 1–30. Academic Press, London.

—— (1977b). Individual differences. In *Child Psychiatry: Modern Approaches,* (eds. Rutter, M. & Hersov, L.) pp. 3–21. Blackwell Scientific Publications. Oxford.

—— (1978). Diagnostic validity in child psychiatry. *Adv. in Bio. Psychiat.*, **2**, 2–27.

—— (1979). *Changing Youth in a Changing Society.* Rock Carling Monograph. Nuffield Provincial Hospitals Trust, London.

—— (1982). Epidemiological-longitudinal approaches to the study of development. In *The Concept of Development.* (ed. Collins, W. A.). Minnesota Symposium on Child Psychology. Vol. 15, pp. 105–44. Lawrence Erlbaum, Hillsdale, N.J.

—— (1984a). Psychopathology and Development: I Childhood antecedents of adult disorder. *Aus. N. Z. J. Psychiat.* **18**, 225–34.

—— (1984b). Psychopathology and Development: II Childhood experiences and personality development, *ibid,* 314–27.

—— & Garmezy, N. (1983). Developmental psychopathology. In *Socialization, Personality and Social Development, Vol. 4. Handbook of Child Psychology,* (ed. Hetherington, E. M.) *4th Ed.,* pp. 775–911. Wiley, New York.

—— & Graham, P. (1966). Psychiatric disorders in 10- and 11-year-old children. *Proc. Roy. Soc. Med., 59,* 382.

—— & Madge, N. (1976). *Cycles of Disadvantage. A Review of Research.* Heinemann Educational Books, London.

—— & Shaffer, D. (1980). DSM III. A step forward or back in terms of the classification of childhood psychiatric disorder? *J. Amer. Acad. Child. Psychiat.,* **19**, 371–94.

——, Lebovici, S., Eisenberg, L., Sneznevskij, A. V., Sadoun, R., Brooke, E. & Lin, T. (1969). A tri-axial classification of mental disorders in childhood. An international study *J. Child Psychol. Psychiat.,* **10**, 41.

——, Shaffer, D. and Sturge, C. (1975). *A guide to a multiaxial classification scheme for psychiatric disorders in childhood and adolescence.* Institute of Psychiatry, London.

——, Tizard, J. & Whitmore, K. (1970). *Education, Health and Behaviour.* Longman, London.

——, Yule, W. & Graham, P. (1973). Enuresis and behavioural deviance. Some epidemiological considerations. In *Bladder Control and Enuresis. Clinics in Development Medicine,* (eds. Kolvin, I., MacKeith, R. & Meadows, S. R.), Nos. 48/49, chap. 17. Spastics International Medicine Publication. Heinemann, London.

——, Yule, B., Quinton, D., Rowlands, O., Yule, W. & Berger, M. (1975). Attainment and adjustment in two geographic areas. III. Some factors accounting for area differences. *Brit. J. Psychiat.,* **126.** 520.

Sacks, P. V. (1974). Childhood enuresis and adult depression. *Lancet,* I, 508.

Sandler, J. & Joffe, R. (1965). Notes on childhood depression. *Int. J. Psychoanal.,* **46**, 88.

Savage, G. H. & Goodall, E. (1907). *Insanity and Allied Neuroses.* New ed. Cassell, London.

Schapira, K., Roth, M., Kerr, T. A. & Gurney, C. (1972). The prognosis of affective disorders: The differentiation of anxiety states from depressive illness. *Brit. J. Psychiat.,* **121**, 175.

Schless, A. P., Mendels, J. K., Kipperman, A. & Cochrane C. (1974). Depression and hostility. *J. Nerv. Ment. Dis.,* **159**, 91.

Schneider, K. (1959). *Clinical Psychopathology.* Trans, Hamilton, M. W., Grune & Stratton, New York.

Schofield, W. (1959). A comparative study of the personal histories of schizophrenic and non psychiatric patients. *J. Abn. Soc. Psychol.,* **59**, 216.

Schulsinger, F. (1972). Psychopathy, heredity and environment. In *Life History Research in Psychopathology,* (eds. Roff, M., Robins, L. N. and Pollack, M.) *Vol. 2.* pp. 102–19. University of Minnesota Press, Minneapolis.

Scott, P. D. (1960). The treatment of psychopaths. *Brit. Med. J.,* **i**, 1641.

Scott, P. D. (1962). Critical periods in behavioural development. *Science,* **138**, 949.

Segal, H. (1973). Introduction to the Works of Melanie Klein. *Int. Psychoanal. Lib.* Hogarth Press, London.

Shaffer, D. (1975). The association between enuresis and emotional disorder: A review of the literature. In *Bladder Control and Enuresis,* (eds. Kolvin, I., MacKeith, R. & Meadows, S. R.) chap. 16, *Clinics in Developmental Medicine* Nos. 48/49. Spastics International Medicine Pub. Heinemann Medical, London.

Shaffer, D. (1977). Enuresis. In *Child Psychiatry: Modern Approaches,* (eds. Rutter, M. & Hersov, L.) pp. 581–612. Blackwell Scientific Publications, Oxford.

Shepherd, M., Oppenheim, A. N. & Mitchell, S. (1966). Childhood behaviour disorders and the Child Guidance Clinic: An epidemiological study. *J. Child Psychol. Psychiat.,* **7**, 39.

——, —— & —— (1971). *Childhood Behaviour and Mental Health.* University of London Press.

Sim, M. (1968). *Guide to Psychiatry.* 2nd ed. Livingstone, London.

Sims, A. C. P. (1973). Importance of a high tracing rate in long term medical follow-up studies. *Lancet,* **2**, 433.

Smith, S., Hanson, R. & Noble, S. (1974). Social aspects of the battered baby syndrome. *Brit. J. Psychiat.,* **125**, 568.

Spicer, C. C., Hare, E. H. & Slater, E. (1973). Neurotic and psychotic forms of depressive illness: Evidence from the age incidence in a national sample. *Brit. J. Psychiat.,* **123**, 535.

Spitz, R. A. (1946). Anaclitic depression: Genesis of psychiatric condition in early childhood. *Psychoanal. Study Child,* **2**, 313.

Stein, S. & Susser, M. W. (1966). Nocturnal enuresis as a phenomenon of institutions. *Dev. Med. Child. Neurol.,* **8**, 677.

Steinberg, D. (1977). Psychotic disorders of adolescence. In *Child Psychiatry: Modern Approaches* (eds. Rutter, M. & Hersov, L.) pp. 748–70. Blackwell Scientific Publications, Oxford.

Steinberg, D. (1983). *The Clinical Psychiatry of Adolescence. Clinical Work from a Social and Developmental Perspective.* Wiley Series of Studies in Child Psychiatry. Wiley, Chichester.

Stott, D. N. (1965). Congenital indications of delinquency. *Proc. Roy. Soc. Med.* **58**, 703.

—— (1967). Abnormal mothering as a cause of mental subnormality. I. A critique of some classic studies of maternal deprivation in the light of possible congenital factors. *J. Child Psychol. Psychiat.,* **3**, 79.

Sullivan, H. S. (1955). *Conceptions of Modern Psychiatry.* Tavistock Publications, London.

Sund, A. (1974). Prognostic factors in neurotic illness, *Acta Psychiat. Scand.,* **50**, 90.

Sundby, H. S. & Kreyberg, P. C. (1968). *Prognosis in Child Psychiatry.* Universitetsförlaget; Oslo: Williams & Wilkins, Baltimore.

Szasz, T. S. (1971). *The Manufacturers of Madness.* Routledge & Kegan Paul, London.

Tennant, C. & Bebbington, P. (1978). The social causation of depression: A critique of the work of Brown and his colleagues. *Psychol. Med.,* **8**, 565–75.

Thom, D. A. & Johnston, F. S. (1941). Time as a factor in the solution of delinquency. *Mental Hygiene,* **25**, 269 (cited by O'Neal & Robins, 1958).

Thomas, A., Chess, S., Birch, H. G., Hertzig, M. E. & Korn, S. (1963). *Behavioural Individuality in Early Childhood.* University of London Press, London.

Thomas, C. D. (1971). The suicide among us: Habits of nervous tension as potential predictors. *The Johns Hopkins Med. J.,* **129**, (**4**), 190.

—— & Duszynski, K. R. (1974). Closeness to parents and the family constellation in a prospective study of five disease states: Suicide, mental illness, malignant tumours, hypertension and coronary heart disease. *The Johns Hopkins Med. J.,* **134 (5)**, 251.

Tuckman, J. & Regan, R. A. (1967). Size of family and behavioural problems in children. *J. Genet. Psychol.,* **111**, 151.

—— & Youngman, R. (1963). Suicidal risk among attempted suicides. *Public Health Reports,* **75**, 585.

Tyrer, P. (1979). Anxiety states. In *Recent Advances in Clinical Psychiatry,* (ed. Granville-Grossman, K.) pp. 161–84. Churchill Livingstone, Edinburgh.

—— & Alexander, J. (1979). Classification of personality disorder. *Brit. J. Psychiat.* **135**. 163.

—— & Tyrer, S. (1974). School refusal, truancy and neurotic illness. *Psychol. Med.,* **4**, 416–21.

Torgerson, S. (1980). The oral obsessive hysterical personality syndromes. A study of heredity and environmental factors by means of the Twin Method. *Arch. Gen. Psychiat.,* **37**, 1272.

van Stockert, F. G. (1956). Psychosen in Kindersalter. *Jb. Jungenpsychiat.,* **1**, 223 (cited by Annell, 1969).

Wallston, B. (1973). The effect of maternal employment on children. *J. Child Psychol. Psychiat.,* **14**, 81.

Walton, H. J. & Presley, A. S. (1973). Use of a category system in the diagnosis of abnormal personality. *Brit. J. Psychiat.,* **122**, 259.

Wardell, W. I. & Balinson, C. B. (1964). Problems encountered in behavioural science research in epidemiological studies. *Amer. J. Publ. Health.* **54**, 972.

Wardle, C. J. (1961). Two generations of broken homes in the genesis of conduct and behaviour disorders in childhood. *Brit. Med. J.,* **2**, 349.

Waring, M. & Ricks, D. (1965), Family patterns of children who become adult schizophrenics. *J. Nerv. Ment. Dis.,* **140**, 351.

Warren, W. (1965). A study of adolescent psychiatric in-patients and the outcome six or more years later. I. Clinical history and hospital findings. *J. Child Psychol. Psychiat.,* **6**, 1.

—— (1965). A study of adolescent psychiatric in-patients and the outcome six or more years later. II. The follow-up study. *J. Child. Psychol. Psychiat.,* **6**, 141.

—— (1971). 'You can never plan the future by the past.' The development of child and adolescent psychiatry in England and Wales. *J. Child Psychol. Psychiat.,* **11**, 241.

Weinberg, W. A. & Brumback, R. A. (1976). Mania in childhood. *Amer. J. Dis. Child.* **130**, 380.

Weiss, A. (1973). The importance of human environment for depressive reaction in psycho-organically disturbed children. *Acta Paedopsychiat.,* **40**, 35.

West, C. (1948). *Lectures on the Diseases of Infancy and Childhood.* Longman, London.

West, D. J. (1969). *Present Conduct and Future Delinquency.* Heinemann, London.

—— & Farrington, D. P. (1977). *The Delinquent Way of Life.* Heinemann, London.

Winokur, G. (1972). Types of depressive illness. *Brit. J. Psychiat.,* **120**, 265.

Wing, J. K. (1975). Epidemiology of schizophrenia. In *Contemporary Psychiatry,* (eds. Silvestone, T. & Barraclough, B.) *British Journal of Psychiatry Special Publication No. 9,* pp. 25–31. Headley Bros., Ashford, Kent.

Wittman, M. P. (1944). A study of prodromal factors in mental illness, with special reference to schizophrenia. *Amer. J. Psychiat.,* **100**, 811.

Wittman, M. (1948). Shut in personality type as a prodromal factor in schizophrenia. *J. Clin. Psychol.,* **4**, 211.

Wolff, S. (1961). Symptomatology and outcome of preschool children with behaviour disorders attending a Child Guidance clinic. *J. Child Psychol. Psychiat.,* **2**, 269.

—— (1971). Dimensions and clusters of symptoms in disturbed children. *Brit. J. Psychiat.,* **118**, 421.

—— (1973). *Children Under Stress.* Penguin, Harmondsworth.

Wolkind, S. (1974a). Sex differences in the aetiology of antisocial disorders in children in long term care. *Brit. J. Psychiat.,* **125**, 125.

—— (1974b). The components of affectionless psychopathy in institutionalized children. *J. Child Psychol. Psychiat.,* **15**, 215.

Yarrow, M. R., Campbell, J. D. & Burton, R. V. (1970). Recollections of childhood: A study of retrospective method. *Monogr. Soc. Res. Child Dev.,* **35**, No. 5.

Yudkin, S. & Holme, A. (1963). *Working Mothers and their Children.* Joseph, London.

Zeitlin, H. (1971). *A Study of Children who attended the Children's Department and later the Adult Department of the same Psychiatric Hospital.* M.Phil. Thesis, London University.

Appendix I

The summaries given here are only those referred to in the text. They are therefore not a representative sample of all index cases.

INDEX CASE 3701

Childhood diagnosis: Mixed conduct and emotional disorder
Adult diagnosis: Schizophrenia
Male
Age at first childhood attendance: 11
Referred in childhood for refusal to go to school. Presenting initially with vomiting. Showed tempers, anxiety, and sleep disturbance, also noted to be stealing. Several episodes of falling limply to the ground. Said to have chronic eye trouble though nature not specified.
Age at first adult attendance: 39.
Follow-up to age 40. Referred for inability to cope. Said to be depressed and show somatic complaints. Described as 'a strange person repeating many symptoms of paranoid schizophrenia as if by rote'. Symptoms include delusions, hallucinations, and possibly thought disorder. Prior to admission found dropping lighted matches in a cupboard in his lodgings. Single, living alone.
Comment: The childhood notes characterize the disturbance as school refusal with a mixture of conduct and neurotic disorder. There is unfortunately scanty information about relationships. In adult life the symptomatology taken at face value would clearly indicate schizophrenia, though the case notes record some doubt as to whether these are real or learned symptoms. The isolation and inability to cope were doubted.

INDEX CASE 3921

Childhood diagnosis: Schizophrenia
Adult diagnosis: Manic depressive
Female
Age at first childhood attendance: 14
Said to have a sudden onset with (secondhand) report of a fit. This was followed by a period of malaise, fever, nausea, and abdominal pain. Said to be rambling, but improved over one week. Seen in psychiatric departments towards the end of this time. Described as gay one day, depressed the next. Claimed that the radio was jumbled up. . . and that it gave clues about her performance as 'Winnie' (not her name).

Age at first adult attendance: 23.
Having episodes of irritability, restlessness and overactivity, alternating with depression, poor appetite, and weight loss. Between episodes, normal mental health and working; aware of the recurring nature of her illness.
Comment: Agreement between case-note diagnoses and research diagnoses in childhood and adult life. The contemporary diagnostician in her childhood does not quite commit himself, talking of an illness with a schizophrenic flavour. There is again an acute onset with an apparent organic illness. In adult life, the records cover twenty years and the pattern is very consistent, with no doubt in the later clinician's mind about diagnosis.

INDEX CASE 4621

Childhood diagnosis: Conduct disorder
Adult diagnosis: Schizophrenia
Female
Age at first childhood attendance: 15
Ran away from home; stealing money. Quiet, stubborn child from birth, always seclusive, unaffectionate to family. Average school performance—always shy and solitary. Commenced running away from home, sometimes for several hours, sometimes for several days taking money varying between ten shillings and eight pounds. Odd, inappropriate smiling.
   Physically normal–mental state uncommunicative. Admitted to the ward and gradually became more communicative, increased conversation on subjects remote from family relationships. Psychological testing showed her to have IQ of 77.
Age at first adult attendance: 35.
Living with mother–no major psychiatric symptoms for 16 years after childhood attendance, then became apathetic, keeping to herself, falling on the floor, pulling her hair out. Occasionaly sitting staring into space, neglecting herself, suspicious, and hostile to mother. Unable to continue occupation of domestic work.
Comment: Childhood mixture of emotional and conduct disorder, though only conduct disorder presented as a problem. Noted also to be an odd girl. Stable with domestic job until employer moved, then onset of overt psychosis in adult life.

INDEX CASE 4622

Childhood diagnosis: Mixed conduct and emotional disorder
Adult diagnosis: Sexual deviation and inadequate personality disorder
Male
Age at first childhood attendance: 15
Presenting with aggressive behaviour towards mother and difficult conduct. Father said to be eccentric and obsessional–mother 'highly strung actress'. Parents separated when subject was aged 7. Mixture of aggressive, hostile behaviour on any frustration, at other times said to be self-conscious and shy of strangers. Obsessionally tidy, anxious, and variety of physical symptoms. Admitted to chil-

dren's ward–investigations–IQ 117. There was no real improvement during admission.

Age at first adult attendance: 20

Admissions continued to age of 38. Married at age 21, subsequently divorced, described as affectionless, said to be immature and irresponsible. Two charges of sexual assault–one assault described as pulling at a child's pants in church, said to be obsessional and anxious.

Comment: Family disruption, and aggressive behaviour continuity on to personality disorder with obsessional continuity also being present.

INDEX CASE 4623

Childhood diagnosis: Conduct disorder and developmental disorder
Adult diagnosis: Schizophrenia
Male
Age at first childhood attendance: 14

Referred in childhood for running away from residential school. Said to be depressed, jealous of stepfather and very unhappy at school.

When picked up by the police, gave story of kidnapping and sexual assault. Thought to be untrue. Noted to show lying, difficult behaviour at school, disturbed relationships with both parents, and developmental disorder. Slight deafness but noted speech and comprehension difficulties. Mental state given as a little hard of hearing, speech hesitant, and monotonous with some lisping, well orientated, normal memory, no abnormal emotional traits. Said to be chess champion at school. No formal psychometric assessment carried out.

Age at first adult attendance: 21

Follow-up to age 36. Referred for depression. Said to have made suicidal attempts, to be apathetic, irritable, sometimes violent. Unable to cope. Dependent. Frequent changes of job. Difficulty in forming relationships. Homosexuality. Noted to show thought disorder, delusions, hallucinations, and incongruous behaviour.

Comment: Unhappy deaf child whose main presenting problem was absconding from school. Also had developmental difficulties regarding speech, language and hearing. Adult record contains letter with typical schizophrenic thought disorder.

INDEX CASE 4703

Childhood diagnosis: Conduct disorder and developmental delay
Adult diagnosis: Unspecified psychosis and immature personality disorder
Male
Age at first childhood attendance: 4

Initially seen for severe motor speech defect and said to be overactive, aggressive with temper tantrums. Attended irregularly from age 4–5. Seen again age 15. Still showing motor-speech difficulties. Three-year history of pains in his throat, one year depression and suicidal threats, three week history of attacks of trembling and dizziness. Said to spend excessive time combing his hair. Generally self-conscious and unhappy, lonely and solitary, fears of failure.

Delivered at term. Precipitate delivery. Birth weight 5 lbs. Well in neo-natal period. Milestones all said to be late. Age 13 months to 15 months diagnosed as 'advanced rickets'. Aged 8 taken into care because of 'filthy and unsatisfactory home conditions'. Aged 12–15 ESN school. At age 15 described as well built, muscular physique, moderate speech defect but intelligible. Anxious and self-conscious. Hypochondriacal preoccupation with throat and speech defect. Notes also record episode of violence to parents and other children and outburst of prolonged laughter. IQ Merrill Palmer 100.
Age at first adult attendance: 17
Follow-up to age 21. Initial referral for persistent enuresis. Noted to be depressed and suicidal. Hypochondrial, said to have delusions of being followed and also ideas of reference. Unable to cope, poor concentration. Socially isolated, living in digs or hostel. Work as labourer with frequent changes. IQ Mill Hill and Matrices 75.
Comment: In childhood an odd, difficult child with marked developmental delay. Severe social and material deprivation. Considerable doubt about precise adult diagnosis, but delusions seem not be be in doubt.

INDEX CASE 4723

Childhood diagnosis: Conduct disorder
Adult diagnosis: Manic-depressive psychosis
Male
Age at first childhood attendance: 10
Age 6, unconscious for 20 minutes after a fall. 48 hours later, unconsciousness for several minutes. Subsequently noted to have periods of irritability. Age 7 found to have central scotoma of the right eye. Age 9–10 two epileptic fits. Subsequently said to tell fantastic stories and at times to be mildly excited. Complained that other boys were against him, and of periodic blackouts. Stole money to buy razor blades and found to have cuts on head. Three weeks before childhood admission became excitable and uncontrollable, losing his temper regularly, complaining of giddiness. Shouting abuse at mother and neighbours and refusing food. Threatened to burn the house down and attacked mother with a pitchfork. On admission to hospital found to be subdued at first but then became active and boisterous. IQ 109. Serial EEGs irregular slow activity suggestive of 'post convulsive state'. Last EEG showed epileptic focus. Behaviour showed steady improvement during in-patient admission.
Age at first adult attendance: 25
Follow-up to age 33. Referred as adult for overactivity. Generally anxious and restless. Began to buy numerous newspapers. Three days before admission became agitated. On admission complained that his brain was 'turning over' and that he had to keep walking and concentrate on music. Complains of swings from elation to depression. Depressive phase includes depressed mood, sleep disturbance, impaired appetite, weight disturbance. Subsequent depressive episode two years after first adult admission. As adult single, living with parents. Working as a salesman with few changes in occupation. Repeat IQ 105.
Comment: The diagnosis of manic-depressive psychosis did not become clear until the information was available from subsequent adult attendances. The child-

hood data might be seen to fit in with the same illness but the assessors did not make reference to the adult data at the time of examining the childhood records. On that evidence alone, manic-depressive psychosis was not diagnosed.

INDEX CASE 4801

Childhood diagnosis: Conduct disorder and encopresis
Adult diagnosis: Depressive neurosis
Male
Age at first childhood attendance: 5
Presented with soiling and smearing, and was said otherwise to be stubborn, sulky and resentful, disobedient and to show temper tantrums.
Said to be defiant to his mother, to the extent of 'making her want to kill him'.
Age at first adult attendance: 20
Presenting with somatic pains and showing depressed mood, sleep disturbance, lassitude, headaches, and anxiety. These had been present for some 10 months by the time of referral. It was noted that he still had a poor relationship with his mother and felt that she had rejected him. He had left home, had a girlfriend and was working as an apprentice engineer.
Comment: This was one of the cases that appeared to show conduct disorder in childhood and normal personality without pyschosis as an adult. There was certainly every indication of normal personality as an adult. However, in childhood, in spite of the complaints of his conduct by his mother the examining psychiatrist described him as a pleasant and agreeable little chap.

INDEX CASE 4804

Childhood diagnosis: Conduct disorder and developmental disorder
Adult diagnosis: Schizophrenia and sexual deviation
Male
Age at first childhood attendance: 10
Referred for backwardness and emotional problems. Described as sly, deceitful boy with tics. Truanting from school, showing bizarre behaviour. Found dancing in the street. Said to have periods of absence, but EEG normal. Attention seeking, few friends. Said to be difficult in school–sulky, restless, disobedient and showed temper tantrums. Also noted to have somatic complaints, tension habits, poor concentration. Isolated from peers. Noted to show educational delay. IQ 103. Court case during childhood for assault by homosexual.
Age at first adult attendance 22.
Follow-up to age 33. Referred in adult life for incongruous behaviour. Said to show initially two-week history of withdrawn behaviour, aimless wandering, muttering incoherently. When seen, described as semi-mute, living with parents. Subsequent admission seeking treatment for homosexuality.
Comment: Apart from the thought disorder and posturing there is remarkable similarity between the childhood and adult records, though the childhood record contains no diagnostic symptom for schizophrenia.

INDEX CASE 4823

Childhood diagnosis: Obsessive and compulsive neurosis and conduct disorder
Adult diagnosis: Obsessive compulsive neurosis
Male
Age at first childhood attendance: 8
Referred during childhood for blinking eyes, also complaining of 'strange thoughts coming into his mind'. Said to be an anxious boy, restless and fidgety. Aggressive and disobedient at school and to mother at home. IQ 110.
Age at first adult attendance: 26
Follow-up to age 30. Referred as adult for anxiety, persistent fears of death, and paralysis. Recent fears of contamination by oil, feels that it might get into his body and that he might die. Knows that it was ridiculous. Also developed panic attacks in crowds and open spaces. Single, living with parents, working as skilled mechanic. Repeat IQ 126.
Comment: The obsessional thoughts in adult life appeared more clearly formulated than those in childhood. The aggressive behaviour appears to have subsided and he made satisfactory work adjustment. He was, however, still dependent on his parents.

INDEX CASE 4921

Childhood diagnosis: Conduct disorder and developmental disorder
Adult diagnosis: Schizophrenia and antisocial personality
Male
Age at first childhood attendance: 8
Referred in childhood for truanting. Wandering away from home at age 4. Ran away from school at first attendance. Since then extensive wanderings–usually by main-line train. Taken into care as being beyond control. Settled there and returned home after 18 months. Wandering behaviour recommenced after one month. Makes extraordinary fantasy stories. Described as showing oddities in thought that have no relevance to immediate subject matter. Also said to show tension habits, isolated from peers, bullied, fidgety and restless. Developmental disorder of delayed speech. Notes describe him as 'like plate glass with reference to rapport'. IQ full scale 93. Arithmetic 2 years retarded for age. Treated with intensive psychotherapy.
Age at first adult attendance: 25
Follow-up to one year. Referred in adult life for forgetfulness. Said to apathetic, unable to cope, dependent, immature, frequent prison sentences for petty offences. Delusional ideas. Describes thoughts as 'going into a little coma'. Socially: single, living alone. Unskilled work. Frequent changes of occupation.
Comment: Similarity between childhood and adult notes except for absence of theft and of first rank symptoms of schizophrenia. Mother's description of his replies are not unlike some aspects of thought disorder. Though the childhood record contains speculation about diagnosis, psychogenic factors were considered most important.

INDEX CASE 5001

Childhood diagnosis: Depression and delinquency
Adult diagnosis: Depression and personality disorder
Male
Age at first childhood attendance: 12
Referred for stealing. Four-year history of various delinquent acts including steal-ing, truanting, lying, violence. Noted also to be sulky, resentful, restless, dis-obedient. Said to be an anxious boy dependent on his mother, showing anxiety sleep disturbance, fears and tension habits. IQ 107. Noted to show educational delay.
Age at first adult attendance 26.
Referred for moodiness and irritability. Said to show depression, anxiety and sleep disturbance. Two suicidal attempts noted. Said also to be violent and aggressive. Criminal record (reason unknown). Working as 'sewer flusher'. Divorced and co-habiting. Described as usually miserable.
Comment: Described as one of four cases showing both neurotic and delinquent disorders in childhod. Neurotic disorder refers to depression; both patterns appear to have continued into adult life.

INDEX CASE 5002

Childhood diagnosis: Unspecified emotional disorder
Adult diagnosis: Unclassified neurosis
Female
Age at first childhood attendance: 10
Complaining of sleeplessness, fits of crying, anxiety about sexual information and fears of being poisoned by the doctor. Said to have started after a recent head injury. Generally noted to have tempers, to be stubborn, get on poorly with peers, be very timid, and to be attention seeking. Considerable parental concern over physical health for many years. All symptoms cleared with 'therapeutic interviews'.
Age at first adult attendance: 23
Referred for depression following the birth of first child. Complaining of fears of dying, fears of germs and infection, also has obsessions concerning cleanliness. Refusing to let the child be touched. Fluctuating course over a period of four months. Married, working as a clerk, said to be psychiatrically well apart from this episode.
Comment: Both in childhood and in adult life, the diagnosis appears to be given of unclassified neurosis because of the mixture of neurotic symptoms, though, in retrospect, there is similarity between the childhood fears and the adult symp-toms later thought to be obsessional. These are not recognized as such at the time of childhood attendance. This is one of three cases in which histrionic behaviour in childhood was not followed by personality disorder in adult life.

INDEX CASE 5103

Childhood diagnosis: Mixed conduct and emotional disorder
Adult diagnosis: Depressive neurosis and antisocial personality disorder
Male
Age at first childhood attendance: 5
Referred in childhood for screaming on frustration. Described as an anxious, timid, isolated child showing excessive masturbation and screaming attacks. Bites his nails, bangs and moves his head, aggressive towards his mother. Deterioration over 6 months, frequent screaming attacks, more withdrawn, playing by himself. Meticulous over food, cleans every speck off a knife, refuses to eat in restaurants because of concern over cleanliness of utensils. Mother described as unstable, hysterical personality, with frequent transient depressions. Said to be immature and show ambivalence towards husband and child.
Age at first adult attendance: 17
Follow-up to age 21. Referred in adult life for aggressive outbursts. Described as anxious, with obsessional fears. Treated in the day hospital. Said at first to be disorderly and aggressive, making crude sexual comments to female patients. Also noted to be depressed, lacking in confidence and dependent. Difficulty in making relationships and unable to get a girlfriend. Single, living alone, working as a laboratory assistant. IQ Verbal 123, Performance 111.
Comment: Though obsessional symptoms are said to be present both in childhood and adult life, they are not the predominant symptoms at any time.

INDEX CASE 5209

Childhood diagnosis: Mixed emotional and conduct disorder
Adult diagnosis: Obsessive, compulsive neurosis and inadequate personality disorder
Male
Age at first childhood attendance: 8
Described as a boy of low intelligence with an anxious single mother. Child said to be timid, reluctant to go out, persistent preoccupation with politics and germs. Persistently cautious about cleanliness for fear of contamination. Behavioural problems at school, also lying to mother, and occasional stealing.
Age at first adult attendance: 20
Working as a packer, living with his mother who is said to be depressed. Complaining of various fears, disturbed sleep, anxiety, irritability and tempers. Obsessional behaviour concerning cleanliness and clothes.
Comment: Shows again the independent continuity of different types of symptom.

INDEX CASE 5221

Childhood diagnosis: Emotional disorder (school refusal)
Adult diagnosis: Antisocial personality disorder
Male
Age at first childhood attendance: 5
Referred for school refusal–manifest on transfer from infants to primary school.

Refused attendance on third day. On following day had epileptic fit with fever. Generally described as restless sleeper, blushes easily, sucks fingers. Preoccupied with fears of school, excitable and aggressive, temper tantrums. At 18 months one fit with fever. Protracted labour, otherwise normal neo-natal period. Development normal. IQ 131. No account of antisocial behaviour during childhood.

Age at first adult attendance: 20
Referred for 'being unable to cope'. Had gone to university and progressed at first. Got into debt and sold family possessions to pay debts. Procured abortion for at least one girlfriend. Became anxious prior to exams. Eventually suspended from university for one year. Since then, numerous jobs. Described as unreliable and untruthful.

Comment: There is evidence of anger but not violence in childhood. For the adult diagnosis the two assessors initially disagreed between immature personality and antisocial, eventually deciding on the latter. There was, however, no overt violence or theft and no court record. There was agreement between assessors and the contemporary record that no formal psychiatric illness was present.

INDEX CASE 5303

Childhood diagnosis: Unspecified emotional disorder and enuresis
Adult diagnosis: Anxiety neurosis and alcoholism
Male
Age at first childhood attendance: 12
Referred with reluctance to go to school, waking at night, crying, pains in the chest, temper tantrums. Given anaesthetic one year previously; since then commenced to refuse school and fears of choking. Described as a frail and happy boy also with fears of people looking at him and of the dark. Obsessional behaviour concerning cleanliness of eating utensils. Other symptoms include tempers, anxiety, depression, sleep disturbance and bed wetting.

Age at first adult attendance: 22
Three year history of fear of dying. Generalized anxiety, feeling of being unable to breathe. Panic attacks in lifts and trains. Still showing obsessional behaviour similar to that exhibited in childhood. Drinking heavily 'to relieve anxiety'.

Comment: Obsessional behaviour at both attendances not reflected in the diagnostic labels.

INDEX CASE 5401

Childhood diagnosis: Emotional disorder and developmental delay
Adult diagnosis: Antisocial personality disorder
Male
Age at first childhood attendance: 9
Referred for backwardness and fears. Described as immature, always acting, never using his natural voice, unable to read or write properly. Said to be awkward in his movements, unable to hold a cup, jerky and impulsive, nail-biter, timid, girlish. Did not enjoy organized games, solitary. Fear of strangers. Behaviour at school described as 'excellent'. No family problems. Older and younger

brothers 'maladjusted'. In early infancy, 'tongue snipped for being tongue-tied'. Early feeding difficulties. Sat at one year, walked at $2\frac{1}{2}$ years, talked after 5 years. Age 6 said to be ESN. On examination, small bilateral inguinal herniorrhaphy scars, slight choreiform movements of hands. Clean, tidy, shy at first, but mischievous later. IQ WISC Performance 89, Verbal 82. During childhood no evidence for antisocial or aggressive behaviour.
Age at first adult atttendance: 23.
Referred for physical aggression to his wife. Married, now separated, physical violence and sexual difficulties during marriage, no children, currently living with parents. Frequent changes of occupation, unskilled work only, no court record. Isolated from peers, limited interests.
Comment: The violence in adult life seem specifically to have been directed against his wife and possibly parents. The childhood records clearly indicate an absence of aggressive or other antisocial behaviour but are characterized by marked developmental delay. The record as a whole would tend to indicate a lifelong incompetence and inability to cope.

INDEX CASE 5403

Childhood diagnosis: Manic-depressive
Adult diagnosis: Schizophrenia
Female
Age at first childhood attendance: 15
Pubertal girl. Preoccupied with sex. Became withdrawn and uninterested, claiming that she did not love God and that she had no feelings. On admission, found to be quiet and withdrawn; described as retarded but fidgety. Later described as agitated and complaining of feelings of guilt. No change of appetite but improved sleep during admission.
Age at first adult attendance: 19.
After 4 years of good health with academic success in 'A' levels at school, became withdrawn. Found to be slow at work and at eating, and to be giggly. Denied depression. Delusions concerning other patients and ideas of reference. Attendance with continuing illness, records covering subsequent six years.
Comment: Case-note records agree with research diagnoses, except that at one point contemporary clinician described adult illness as 'schizophrenia with affective element'. None the less, the decreasing affective context seems to have been the main reason for change of diagnosis.

INDEX CASE 5404

Childhood diagnosis: Emotional disorder
Adult diagnosis: Personality disorder (immature)
Female
Age at first childhood attendance: 15
Referred with panic attacks. Six months sudden onset of various fears, mainly of dying; said to be histrionic and attention seeking, stubborn but dependent. Suffers from pulmonary TB.

Age at first adult attendance: 24
Presented with phobias, obsessions and anxieties. Also noted to be depressed with disturbance of appetite and sleep. Said to show aggressive outbursts, which were manifest also whilst in-patient and directed towards staff.
Comment: One of the index cases showing obsessions for the first time in adult life. Presence of the symptom not reflected in the diagnostic label. Aggressive behaviour in female with 'immature personality disorder'.

INDEX CASE 5502

Childhood diagnosis: Emotional disorder
Adult diagnosis: Schizophrenia
Male
Age at first childhood attendance: 12
Referred in childhood for fear of mixing with other people. Three weeks' refusal to go to school. Seems unhappy but unable to say why. Frequent complaints of stomach aches, enuresis to age 8. Fears of the dark. Emotionally described as unhappy, submissive, but resentful of being so. Unable to concentrate. No friends. No antisocial behaviour. No developmental problems. IQ verbal 124, Performance 106.
Age at first adult attendance: 21
Follow-up to age 27. Referred initially for suicidal attempt. Several subsequent admissions. Complains of depression, becomes withdrawn with suicidal thoughts. Feels persecuted by workmen in the street. Believes that they can read his thoughts. Persistent thoughts to pluck out his own eyes. Some hand-washing rituals, unable to hold a job, ambivalent sexual orientation, isolated episodes of aggressive and violent behaviour.
Comment: Contemporary childhood notes give no suspicion about future psychotic illness. Described as 'serious neurosis, the aggressive anal and obsessive elements being clear'.

INDEX CASE 5504

Childhood diagnosis: Emotional disorder and developmental disorder
Adult diagnosis: Personality disorder (immature)
Female
Age at first childhood attendance: 9
Presenting with clumsiness, anxious, with various fears of dogs, travelling, being chased. Bullied at school. Said to be noticeably clumsy and fidgety. IQ verbal 94, Performance 64. EEG said to be abnormal.
Age at first adult attendance: 18.
Living with mother, unemployed. No friends, no outside interests, said to be overactive and showing outbursts of violence against family. Expressing fears of getting pregnant.
Comment: One of the cases showing no (recorded) evidence for aggression or other antisocial behaviour, who show violence in adult life. Clumsiness, fidgetiness, and verbal/performance discrepancies on IQ test in childhood suggest some organic dysfunction.

INDEX CASE 5710

Childhood diagnosis: Emotional disorder
Adult diagnosis: Antisocial personality disorder
Male
Age at first childhood attendance: 11
Referred for school refusal. Attended new school for 14 days, followed by 5 weeks' absence for knee infection then refusal to go to school with multiple somatic complaints. Generally anxious, with complaints of abdominal pain, anxiety, vomiting, sleep difficulties. Described as tense, overtalkative, finger-picking and nose-picking. Obedient, clinging and dependent on mother. More interested in play with girls than boys. Unplanned pregnancy, attempt at abortion. Milestones: normal. On examination, fair-haired, bright, pleasant anxious about mother. WISC full scale IQ 114. No recorded evidence for violence or aggression.
Age at first adult attendance: 18
Referred for indecent exposure. Homosexual activities in public lavatory. Irritable, isolated, miserable. Charged with stealing, employed as solicitor's clerk
Comment: No record of any antisocial or aggressive behaviour in childhood except for some anger against father. Unanimous agreement, in all diagnosis in adult life, about antisocial personality disorder. This is the only case in which there is such a clear divergence between the absence of delinquent behaviour in childhood and its presence in adult life.

INDEX CASE 5803

Childhood diagnosis: Schizophrenia
Adult diagnosis: Personality disorder
Male
Age at first childhood attendance: 15
Mother in-patient for mania. Father unknown. Fostered from birth. Age 5–poliomyelitis mainly affecting hands. Age 14–said to have ideas of grandeur of being a footballer. Otherwise described as being popular, cheerful, lazy, easily influenced, and disliking correction. Admitted with a nine-day history of ideas of persecution, being depressed and withdrawn. Mental state: 'Talk rambling, inconsequential, showing thought disorder'. Confused, disorientated and anxious. Thought to be visually hallucinated.
Age at first adult attendance: 21
Single, living alone, and out of work. Unable to cope, depressed, and violent. Notes, however, record doubt concerning diagnosis of personality disorder or psychosis.
Comment: The case-notes record affective psychosis in childhood and personality disorder in adult life. Some suggestion of organic basis in childhood.

INDEX CASE 5804

Childhood diagnosis: Schizophrenia
Adult diagnosis: Manic-depressive
Female

Age at first childhood attendance: 15
Two years–periods of excitement, overtalkativeness, irritability and sleepiness each lasting about two weeks. In one month noted to have excitement followed by depression. On admission, tall, thin, pubertal girl. Puzzled, vague. Depressed and apathetic, though this fluctuated. Answers off the point. Felt that doctors and nurses were not what they claimed to be. Thought her hair had lice.
Age at first adult attendance: 17
After interval of good health, readmitted with similar symptoms. After commencing chlorpromazine said to have shown clear mood swings with periodicity of six weeks. When last seen was still having mood swings, some six years after the initial admission.
Comment: The case notes gave the same diagnosis in childhood and adult life as the research assessment. In childhood the history alone may have given a diagnosis of manic-depressive illness, but the findings on examination indicated a diagnosis of schizophrenia. Subsequently, the periodicity with intervals of good health seem to have been the principal factors in the diagnosis of manic-depressive illness.

INDEX CASE 5807

Childhood diagnosis: Schizophrenia
Adult diagnosis: Manic-depressive psychosis
Male
Age at first childhood attendance: 14
At unspecified age had a 'fit' during a febrile illness followed by confused behaviour. For five weeks prior to admission became excited. Described as having flight of ideas and ideas of reference. Found to be anxious, apprehensive, and perplexed. Negativism.
Age at first adult attendance: 17
Three admissions subsequently up to age 21.
(1) 'Fit' followed by agitation, difficulty in sleeping. Delusions of darts and arrows being fired by the Pope.
(2) Agitated, grandiose. 'I am Jesus . . . I own the world'. Overactive.
(3) Gave up work whilst feeling elated. Two days later depressed. Felt that objects had a special meaning for him.
Comment: In this case the case notes record toxic psychosis as the diagnosis at age 14; had periodic catatonic schizophrenia at the final admission. As with case 5803, there was considerable discussion, including a special case conference to try to classify the illness. The participants at the latter gave varying diagnoses from temporal lobe epilepsy (EEG normal) to repressed homosexuality. The strong organic flavour is noted, but also the periods of good mental health between episodes, the periodicity, and the marked swings of mood.

INDEX CASE 5808

Childhood diagnosis: Emotional disorder and delinquency
Adult diagnosis: Schizophrenia and personality disorder
Male

Age at first childhood attendance: 13
Referred in childhood as being beyond control. Mother complained of bad language, disobedience, stealing, 'bad company', wanders away, picked up on one occasion by the police. Court appearance for theft. Described as being a quiet, sensitive, well-brought up boy until four months previously. Development normal except delay in walking until 22 months. Still clumsy and poor at practical tasks. Good school record. Described as anxious boy, so dominated that it is causing him 'a good deal of guilt to rebel'. Parents separated, mother one episode of hysterical paralysis, father said to be a 'proper rotter', (ignominious discharge from the services for bad conduct).
Age at first adult attendance: 19
Referred for masturbating in public. One suicidal attempt, drug addiction, convictions for theft, homosexuality, violent attack on mother, previously living in hostels and returned home. Frequent changes of job. During attendance claimed to hear his voice called out and to see a cross in the sky.
Comment: Contemporary case notes give diagnosis uncertain but appear to accept validity of apparent psychotic phenomena. Research assessors argued that 'no personality disorder' could not be recorded and psychotic phenomena could not be discounted. Motor developmental disorder noted in childhood but not designated as diagnosis.

INDEX CASE 5809

Childhood diagnosis: Emotional disorder
Adult diagnosis: Anxiety neurosis and personality disorder
Male
Age at first childhood attendance: 14
An anxious child presenting with refusal to go to school. Said to be dependent, lacking in confidence, and showing somatic complaints, and headaches. IQ 115.
Age at first adult attendance: 19
Presenting with numerous physical complaints. Worked as an apprentice horticulturist, difficulty in holding jobs. Living with parents. Increasing absence from work, drinking alcohol excessively, and aggressive and violent towards family, said generally to have difficulty in coping and to be immature.
Comment: Bright boy presenting with school refusal and emotional disorder with somatic symptoms. As adult, aggressive behaviour with work and relationship difficulties.

INDEX CASE 5926

Childhood diagnosis: Conduct disorder and enuresis
Adult diagnosis: Manic-depressive
Female
Age at first childhood attendance: 13
Referred for aggressive behaviour. Said to have outbursts of violent temper with aggressiveness and destructiveness. Tried to hang herself and set fire to clothes. Also shows lying, difficult behaviour in school, moodiness, and disobedience. Complains of depression. Suffers from grand mal epilepsy and also enuretic.

Between outbursts, described as friendly, social, immature little girl. Separated from parents at the age of 2, then lived with foster parents until foster father charged with indecent assault on ESN sister-in-law. IQ Verbal 113, Performance 87.
Age at first adult attendance: 21
Follow-up to age 23. Referred for depression. Complaining of misery, sleep disturbance, impaired appetite, and suicidal attempts. Noted to be irritable and unable to cope. Recent self-neglect. Admitted to hospital following overdose. On recovery found to be talkative, active displaying pressure of thought. Review of history suggests several previous episodes of hypomania following depressive phases. Epilepsy reasonably well controlled throughout. Medication: Valium, Lithium, Mysoline and Epanutin. Married, one child, apparently stable home life. Repeat IQ testing Verbal 103, Performance 80.
Comment: The social environment during childhood was chaotic and from the childhood record there seemed adequate evidence to account for the aggression and depression. Subsequent to the childhood attendance there seems to have been sufficient stability to marry and maintain a home.

INDEX CASE 6029

Childhood diagnosis: Conduct disorder and sexual deviation
Adult diagnosis: Depression
Female
Age at first childhood attendance: 13
Referred by Probation Officer. Complaints of undisciplined for three years, temper tantrums of highly dramatic nature, abusive to mother, wearing tight skirts, sexual promiscuity. Good school report. Natural father died when child aged six months, now has good relationship with stepfather. Treated in adolescent ward. On admission described as 'considerable facade'. IQ Performance 129, Verbal 111.
Age at first adult attendance: 20.
Referred for depression. Several bouts of depression with suicidal attempts. Several histrionic outburts, sleeping poorly, said to show apathy and anxiety. Histrionic outbursts continued from time to time. Living at home with mother and stepfather. Steady job as clerk.
Comment: In childhood showed various features almost exclusively associated with an outcome of personality disorder, including court appearance and histrionic and attention-seeking behaviour.

INDEX CASE 6121

Childhood diagnosis: Manic-depressive
Adult diagnosis: Manic-depressive
Female
Age at first childhood attendance: 13
One year previously, depressed for several days, said this was because she had no friends. One month before admission depressed for one week, claims to have seen notes on teacher's desk with adverse comments. Ten days prior to admission

depressed again, sleeping poorly, appetite diminished, became slow, expressing odd ideas, feelings of guilt, and self-reproach. Previously described as reserved, but happy; poor mixer, conscientious. No antisocial behaviour, menarche age 12. Father aged 53–barrister, onset of schizophrenia 13 years ago, slow deterioration, now unpredictable. Mother, 38–doctor. Said to be tall, well-developed, attractive girl, depressed and retarded, ideas of reference, feelings of guilt and self-reproach, seeming bewildered and perplexed. WISC level 129, Performance 119. Remained unchanged for four days then showed rapid improvement over 48 hours. No further signs of disorder during admission.

Age at first adult attendance: 18

Admitted to bouts of depression approximately twice a year since childhood admission, each usually also associated with a period of excitement and over-activity. One year before admission expressed ideas that teachers and pupils at school against her. Five months before admission episode of inappropriate giggling followed by depression, treated with amitriptyline. Gradual increase in weight. On admission depressed, restless, apathetic, unable to do school work, sleeping poorly at night. Admission followed by spontaneous improvement over several days. Re-admitted six months later. During interval successfully took 'A' level French. Proceeded to work as receptionist to general practitioner. One month before admission became overactive and enthusiastic, gradually worsening. Became unconcerned about appearance and impaired sleep. Developed paranoid ideas about mother. Improvement on chloropromazine, subsequently commenced on Lithium. Out-patient follow-up over two years. No further recurrence. Last recorded note: pleasant, intelligent, planning to get married.

Comment: Early onset manic-depressive psychosis. Illness characterized by mood change and onset to first diagnosed episode over period of one week.

Appendix II

Diagnostic categories used for child and adult records
Classification of disorders
General notes

CHILD DIAGNOSTIC CATEGORIES

1. One scale only.
2. 1st and 2nd diagnosis on each–if no 2nd diagnoses 15 on second scale.
3. If two diagnoses are made, that with the lower number is always the first diagnosis.
4. Definitions as in Triaxial classification unless otherwise stated, (Rutter *et al.* 1969) and code numbers refer to this.
5. Manic-depressive illness separated from other psychosis because of possible single grouping of all depressive illness.
6. Delinquency is rated only as category 9 unless there is specific reason to place the subject in another group, eg. neurotic. Where delinquency is diagnosed neither conduct disorder nor mixed disorder can also be diagnosed.

ADULT DIAGNOSTIC CATEGORIES

1. Two scales are used.
   1st diagnosis: Psychiatric 'illness'.
   Six main groups A–F.
   Seventeen individual groups.
2. 2nd diagnosis. Personality disorder. Five groups.
3. Items 15 and 16 of the first diagnostic scale refer to the same items 5 and 4 of the second scale. This enables them to be used in addition to other items on the second scale. If they are present as the only diagnosis then they are scored on the second scale only.
4. Code numbers refer to the Glossary of Mental Disorders, HMSO, 1968, and all definitions are as in that glossary unless otherwise stated.

CHILDHOOD DIAGNOSTIC CATEGORIES

Psychosis
1. Schizophrenia   5.3
   Other psychoses   5.4
2. Manic-depressive psychosis 5.4
3. Infantile psychosis   5.1
   Disintegrative psychosis   5.2

Neurotic disorders

4. Obsessive-compulsive.
5. Anorexia nervosa.
6. All other neurotic disorders, including anxiety, hysterical, phobic depressive, hypochondriacal.
7. Conduct disorders: other than delinquent, including aggression, fighting, overactivity, disobedience.
8. Mixed neurotic and conduct disorder
9. Delinquency: including disorders of conduct resulting in or liable to result in legal intervention; also including any behaviour which would be considered criminal in an adult.
10. Sexual deviation including any abnormality of sexual object, e.g., homo-sexuality, fetishism, also including exhibitionism and exposure.
11. Developmental disorders
    Including hyperkinetic syndrome 2.1
    Speech and language disorder   2.2
    Other specific learning disorder 2.3
    Abnormal clumsiness   2.4
12. Enuresis.
    Encopresis.
13. Tics.
14. Any other psychiatric disorder.
15. No psychiatric disorder. Including adaptation reaction.

Adult diagnostic categories

A. Psychoses.

1. Schizophrenia   295
   Including paranoid states 297
2. Manic-depressive   296
3. Unclassified psychosis   298/299

B. Neuroses. 300

4. Anxiety   300.0
5. Hysterical   300.1
6. Phobic   300.2
7. Obsessive/compulsive 300.3
8. Depressive   300.4
9. Hypochondriacal   300.7
   Including somatic symptoms
10. Depersonalization   300.6
11. Unclassified neurosis 300.8
    Including neurasthenia 300.9
                        300.5

Other psychiatric illness.

12. Organic psychoses 290
    291
    292
    293
    294
13. Psychosomatic disorders 305
14. Other psychiatric illnesses not otherwise included.

D.

15. Sexual deviation 302

E.

16. Alcoholism or addition addiction 303

F.

17. Personality disorder but none of the above.

Personality disorders

1. No personality disorder.
2. Aggressive/antisocial personality disorder.
3. Inadequate/immature/hysterical personality disorder.
4. Alcoholism or other addiction but not 2 or 3.
5. Sexual deviation but not 2, 3, or 4.

Appendix III

Additional tables

Table A1. *Showing age and sex differences for diagnostic categories for index and control boys*

Childhood diagnosis	Overall (N=161)		Boys under 12 (N=71)		Boys under 12 (N=27)	
	Index	Control	Index	Control	Index	Control
Psychosis	10	4	1	1	3	1
	(6.2)	(2.5)	(1.4)	(1.4)	(11.1)	(3.8)
Neurotic only	60	52	21	18	8	8
	(37.3)	(32.3)	(29.6)	(25.0)	(29.5)	(30.6)
Mixed conduct/	32	32	22	11	2	4
neurotic	(19.9)	(19.9)	(31.0)	(15.3)	(7.4)	(15.4)
Delinquency and	58	59	30	33	13	12
conduct	(36.0)	(36.6)	(42.3)	(45.8)	(48.0)	(46.0)
Developmental	33	42	20	27	8	3
disorder	(20.5)	(26.0)	(28.1)	(37.5)	(29.5)	(11.5)
Enuresis/Encopresis	18	40	9	28	2	3
	(11.1)	(24.6)	(12.7)	(39.0)	(7.4)	(11.5)
Other	15	17	5	6	3	6

Table shows raw data, with percentage of each column total given in brackets.

Table A2. *Showing age and sex differences for diagnostic categories for index and control girls*

Childhood diagnosis	Overall (N=161)		Girls under 12 (N=71)		Girls under 12 (N=27)	
	Index	Control	Index	Control	Index	Control
Psychosis	10 *(6.2)*	4 *(2.5)*	0	2 *(6.5)*	6 *(18.8)*	0
Neurotic only	60 *(37.3)*	52 *(32.3)*	14 *(45.0)*	12 *(40.0)*	17 *(53.0)*	14 *(42.5)*
Mixed conduct/ neurotic	32 *(19.9)*	32 *(19.9)*	6 *(19.4)*	9 *(30.0)*	2 *(6.3)*	8 *(24.2)*
Delinquency and conduct	58 *(36.0)*	59 *(36.6)*	8 *(25.8)*	4 *(13.3)*	7 *(21.8)*	10 *(30.4)*
Developmental disorder	33 *(20.5)*	42 *(26.0)*	4 *(12.8)*	6 *(20.0)*	1 *(3.1)*	6 *(18.2)*
Enuresis/Encopresis	18 *(11.1)*	40 *(24.6)*	6 *(19.4)*	7 *(23.3)*	1 *(3.1)*	2 *(6.1)*
Other	15	17	3	2	4	3

Table shows raw data, with percentage of each column total given in brackets.

Table A3. *Items used for discriminant function analysis*

	Male	Female
Abnormal pregnancy/delivery	X	X
Abnormal milestones	X	X
Shyness ⎫	X	X
Anxiety ⎪	X	X
Sombreness ⎬ Recorded as personality	X	X
Reservedness ⎪ characteristic	X	X
Aggressiveness ⎪	X	
Irritability ⎭	X	
Dependency	X	X
Appetite abnormality		X
Educational retardation	X	
Sulkiness		X
Restlessness	X	
Tempers	X	
Obsessions	X	X
Somatic complaints	X	X
Sleep disturbance	X	X
Fears and phobias	X	X
Tension and gratification habits	X	X
Disturbed mother/child relationship	X	X
Peer isolation	X	X
Incongruous behaviour	X	X
Stubborness		X

X selected items for separate analysis on male and female subjects.

Table A4. *Father's social class compared with social class of index cases in adult life*

	Parental social class				
	I & II	III	IV & V	Unemployed	Total
Index case					
I & II	4	3	1	0	8
III	9	41	18	0	68
IV & V	1	30	33	0	64
Unemployed	2	4	5	0	11
Total	16	78	57	0	151

Table A5. *Outcome for children showing only emotional disorder*

Diagnosis at adult attendance	Male	Female
Depression	3	6
Anxiety neurosis	1	2
Phobic neurosis	1	3
Obsessive/compulsive	0	4
Unclassifed neurosis	1	4
Sexual deviation	2	0
P.D. only	1	1
Schizophrenia	1	0
(All with personality disorder)	5	15

Last category includes some from previous categories.

Author index

Subject index